BIBLE STUDY FOR THE 21ST CENTURY

FQ
FAITH
QUEST

A Journey Toward
Congregational Transformation

Dan R. Dick

Acknowledgments

Many people have invested time, energy, and talent in producing both the original FaithQuest Bible study and this reprint.

Thanks to Dan Dick and the original collaborators who developed the content and process of the Bible study.

Thanks to the congregational leaders who have used the Bible study and provided feedback for this reprint. They continue to share experiences and insights to benefit others.

Thanks to national trainers who practice the FaithQuest principles of assessing current reality and living into a future in which congregations are God-centered, faith-forming communities. These leaders are building bridges between current reality and the future.

Thanks to Mike Bealla for collaborating on this reprint and to Joan Newell, who keeps FaithQuest work running smoothly.

—Betsey Heavner
    Director of FaithQuest Strategies for Congregational Leaders

Cover and book design by Sharon Anderson

Edited by Cheryl Capshaw, Linda R. Whited, and David Whitworth

ISBN 0-88177-399-9

Library of Congress Control Number: 2002111442

Scripture quotations, unless otherwise indicated (excluding those within quotations from John Wesley), are from the New Revised Standard Version of the Bible, copyright © 1989 by the Division of Christian Education of the National Council of the Churches of Christ in the USA. All rights reserved. Used by permission.

FAITHQUEST: A Journey Toward Congregational Transformation. Copyright © 1998, 2002 Discipleship Resources. All rights reserved. No part of this book may be reproduced in any form whatsoever, print or electronic, without written permission, except in the case of brief quotations embodied in critical articles or reviews. For information regarding rights and permissions, contact Discipleship Resources, PO Box 340003, Nashville, TN 37203-0003; phone 800-814-7833 (toll-free) or 615-340-7068; fax 615-340-1789; e-mail mgregory@gbod.org.

DR399

Contents

Introduction 5

SECTION 1 THE GOSPEL OF LUKE
A NEW WAY OF THINKING ABOUT JESUS CHRIST 7

- Session 1   A New Paradigm 9
- Session 2   Understanding God's Purpose 19
- Session 3   Doing God's Will 27
- Session 4   Leadership in Turbulent Times 33
- Session 5   The Power of the Resurrection 41

SECTION 2 THE ACTS OF THE APOSTLES
A NEW WAY OF THINKING ABOUT THE CHURCH 49

- Session 6   Life in the Spirit 51
- Session 7   The People We Serve 59
- Session 8   The Road to Transformation 67
- Session 9   Called to Serve 75
- Session 10 To the Ends of the Earth 83

SECTION 3 THE EPISTLE TO THE EPHESIANS
A NEW WAY OF THINKING ABOUT THE WORLD 93

- Session 11 Union With Christ 95
- Session 12 Becoming the Body of Christ 101
- Session 13 New Rules for a New Reality 111

SECTION 4 THE TEACHINGS OF JOHN WESLEY
A NEW WAY OF THINKING ABOUT THE CHRISTIAN LIFE 117

- Session 14 The More Excellent Way 119
- Session 15 The Means of Grace 129
- Session 16 To Spread Scriptural Holiness Across the Land ... 137
- Session 17 The World Is Our Parish 147

Endnotes 157

Introduction

Welcome to *FaithQuest*! You are about to embark on a journey of sharing, learning, and growing in faith with a group of leaders in your congregation. FaithQuest is not a program or single resource. FaithQuest is a process—a journey—for leaders in local churches. Laity and clergy, in both formal leadership positions and informal positions, will benefit from making this journey together. Jesus inaugurated the Christian journey two thousand years ago, and the journey will continue into the future. It is important to learn how to make the faith journey with integrity and effectiveness. This Bible study—*FaithQuest: A Journey Toward Congregational Transformation*—is a step on the journey for twenty-first-century leaders.

Many congregational leaders are seeking ways to transform their local churches. Books on a wide variety of church-growth and leadership topics are available to help with this pursuit. Ultimately, though, many of these books provide information rather than transformation, because they focus on changing the institution rather than on changing lives. The focus on transformation is what makes the FaithQuest Bible study unique.

FaithQuest: A Journey Toward Congregational Transformation is founded upon a single, but important, shift: a movement away from preserving the church as an institution to re-creating the church as faithful community centered in Jesus Christ. The focus of the church is not the church but God. The institution of the church exists to bring people into a healthy relationship with God so that they may live transformed and transforming lives in the world. The church is not a place we visit; it is who we are wherever we live, work, and play. FaithQuest helps us remember why we are the church, and it challenges us to be the best church we can be.

How FaithQuest Works

This Bible study begins with an orientation and continues with the seventeen chapters outlined on the contents page. The sequence of lessons represents a movement first to God, then to the community of faith, then to the world, and finally to what it means individually and collectively to live as Christian disciples in the twenty-first century.

Preparation

Each week, set aside a half-hour a day for personal study and reflection. Begin the study time with prayer, possibly the printed prayer at the beginning of each lesson. Follow the instructions for each day, reading a Scripture passage or lesson material. Keep a notebook or journal to write down anything interesting, confusing, provocative, or new. Read through the "Questions for Reflection" and write your answers and insights.

Exploration

Participants gather weekly for a time of discussion. The outline of the weekly sessions is printed on the first page of each session. It is designed to help small groups maximize the benefits of the study material. It is a simple, straightforward time of learning and sharing and can be modified to meet the needs of each group. Allow two hours for your weekly gathering. You may want to plan more time for refreshments or extended prayer and worship.

Discovery

This is the process of applying the ideas learned to real-life experience and specific congregational settings. As group members move on the journey, they prepare individually for the process, explore the new terrain, and talk about their discoveries along the way. How a group processes the information is as important as the information itself.

The discovery process begins during the weekly group meeting and continues as participants meet with others during regular church gatherings. FaithQuest participants become salt, yeast, and light in the congregation as they lovingly raise questions, tell others about new insights, and learn together. This process invites the FaithQuest participants and ultimately the congregation to be open to the transforming power of God's love and leading.

FaithQuest is intended to be used in the most effective way by each local congregation. It may be modified to meet the changing demands of the church year. The four sections may be scheduled around Advent, Lent, holiday weeks, and special events. The entire study could be completed easily within a single year. Churches may also design day-long retreats for each of the four segments.

Any congregation that works through FaithQuest will be changed for the better. The ideas and insights are not new; they are timeless. For many church leaders, however, they will be a new way of thinking about Jesus Christ, the church, the world, and the Christian life. Once these new ideas are introduced, they are difficult to forget. May God work with you to offer new hope, new energy, and new vitality to your congregation and to your own journey of discipleship. May FaithQuest be a helpful tool for your journey of personal and congregational transformation.

The Role and Function of the Leader

The leader of the FaithQuest Bible study plays a critical role in the success of the process. The leader is to maintain focus and to guide the group on the journey. It is not expected, nor even beneficial, that the leader be "the teacher." Having biblical knowledge and teaching expertise is of secondary importance to facilitating a process of building trust, nurturing faith, creating an atmosphere for sharing and dialogue, and raising appropriate questions along the way. Each member of the group serves as both student and teacher. The study focuses on what the biblical concepts and other ideas mean to the individual, to the group, and to the community of faith.

To facilitate the group process, it is important that the leader be mindful of different learning and interaction styles. Learning styles are the ways that people receive, process, and interpret information. Interaction styles are the ways people learn, work, discuss, and make decisions together.

Leader's Guide at www.faithquest.net

The website has a variety of helps for leaders and is updated continually. You will find:
- an outline for each group meeting;
- suggestions for the focus verse of each group meeting;
- background information on Scripture;
- links to websites on leadership, biblical scholarship, and organizational management;
- suggestions for effective teaching, learning, and group process;
- suggestions for expanding the exploration and discovery phases of FaithQuest;
- reviews of new resources related to FaithQuest.

The FaithQuest Network

While you and your group are experiencing FaithQuest, groups in other congregations will also be meeting. Many congregations have already had Bible study groups. The network provides support for congregations during the time they have active Bible study groups and opportunities for continued learning with your congregation. You can have phone and e-mail connections through the General Board of Discipleship to other FaithQuest congregations. Visit www.faithquest.net to participate in the network. Sign-up for *Leadership Lines and Links*, a monthly electronic newsletter for congregational leaders.

SECTION 1
The Gospel of Luke

A New Way of Thinking About Jesus Christ

Each of the four gospels presents a different picture of Jesus Christ. In Luke's Gospel, Jesus is a champion of the poor, the lost, the broken, and the outcast. He is a champion of justice and righteousness. Jesus confronts the leaders of his day with a new message and a new vision for the people of God.

"A New Way of Thinking About Jesus Christ" is an invitation to meet the Son of God again and to see Jesus in two contexts: the historical context of the Gospel of Luke and the contemporary context of today's church.

SESSION 1: A New Paradigm

Scriptures:
- Luke 1:1–7:50
  Focus Verses: Luke 6:20-26

Key Biblical Concepts:
- Jesus ushers in a new paradigm
- Jesus challenges the existing order and authorities
- Jesus changes the rules
- Jesus teaches in parables

Key Concepts for the Journey:
- Paradigms
- Resistance to change
- New information

Outline:
- Gathering
- A Time of Centering
- Prayer
- Preparation
  Questions and Answers
- Exploration
  A Reflective Moment Along the Way
  Questions and Small-Group Exercises
- Discovery
- Conclusion

Introduction

Many people came claiming to be the Messiah, but only Jesus came bringing a whole new meaning to the title. Jesus challenged existing ideas and institutions, and he proclaimed a new set of rules. Jesus said that he came to stir things up and to bring about the dawn of a new age. In this session, we will look at Jesus, who makes all things new.

Prayer

Creator God, you make all things new. Often, we look at life through eyes that are clouded by what we expect to see. We are closed to new possibilities. We become set in our ways; and when our ways are challenged, we become defensive. Help us to be open to your son, Jesus Christ, who challenges us to see things through new eyes, to hear things through new ears. Help us to broaden our perspectives and to be open to new realities. By your grace, make us a people of endless possibility. We pray in Jesus' holy name. Amen.

Preparation
Daily Scripture References and Questions for Reflection

Day 1 — Luke 1:1–2:38

What are the "extraordinary" occurrences in these passages? How do they challenge your understanding of reality?

_____
_____
_____
_____
_____
_____

FaithQuest: A New Way of Thinking About Jesus Christ

Day 2 — Luke 2:39–3:38
What is the main message of John the Baptist? How do people react to his message?

_____
_____
_____
_____
_____

Day 3 — Luke 4:1-44
What does the devil offer Jesus? What is Jesus' response? What is the main message of Jesus of Nazareth? How do people respond?

_____
_____
_____
_____
_____

Day 4 — Luke 5:1–6:19
In what ways does Jesus challenge the practices and instruction of his time?

_____
_____
_____
_____

Day 5 — Luke 6:20–7:50
List all the "surprising" teachings in Luke 6:20-40. What "new realities" does Jesus introduce through his healings in chapter 7?

_____
_____
_____
_____
_____
_____

Day 6
Read the session material for the weekly group meeting. Begin to reflect on the questions throughout the session material that will be discussed by your group.

Exploration
Background Information: A Different Kind of World

It is difficult to imagine a world without Jesus. The stories of Jesus have become so much a part of our lives that it is nearly impossible to unlearn them. Just think about the incredible impact Jesus had on his time and on the religious hierarchy of the day. Jesus brought a new way of thinking and a new way of teaching to the Jewish faith. His message was so radical that it set the wheels in motion that would crush and destroy him.

The established order of the Jewish faith drew clear lines. The Pharisees were the interpreters of the Law, the Sadducees were the Law keepers, the scribes transmitted the writings of the Law and of the Prophets to all generations, and the priests performed the sacred rites and rituals of the people. Wealth and power were clear signs of the pleasure and providence of God. Poverty was the rule for more than ninety-five percent of the population. The majority of people were uneducated, and they made their living agriculturally or through the performance of a skilled trade. Few people lived into their fourth decade, and virtually no poor person expected the blessing of an afterlife. The Ten Commandments were the Law of the people, and the religious leaders maintained that strict adherence to the Law was the only way to find favor with God. Although people might have to go without food and adequate shelter, there was no question that they would part with their first fruits to provide for the leaders of the Temple. The Jewish leaders of Jesus' day had crafted a complex and sophisticated organizational structure that provided many benefits for the insiders, and it effectively kept outsiders out.

The time was ripe for change. Jesus confronted the religious leaders as no one had before him. With an incredible knowledge of the Scriptures and of the tradition of the Jewish people, Jesus repeatedly disarmed the scribes and Pharisees, and he opened the truth to the common women and men. Jesus uncovered for ordinary people the treasure that the religious hierarchy had protected for themselves. No wonder Jesus was perceived as a threat and was the target of the wrath of the priests, the Sadducees, the Pharisees, and the scribes.

What was it that Jesus said and did that was so radical? A brief survey of any of the gospels will show that virtually *everything* Jesus said was confrontational and provocative. Jesus reversed the perceived roles of the rich and the poor, the humble and the proud, the prestigious and the plain. He made the religious and political leaders look petty and foolish. Jesus attended to the outcasts of his society, often giving preference to their needs over those of the Jewish elite. Jesus reckoned women and children as equals in a culture that offered no respect to either group. Jesus also proclaimed the kingdom of God as a new paradigm, replacing the epoch of the Law and the Prophets.

A Different Kind of Jesus

The author of the Gospel of Luke paints a portrait of a different kind of Jesus than we often imagine. He was certainly not a blond-haired, blue-eyed, soft-featured Savior. The Jesus of Luke is a rough-edged, sharp-tongued rogue who moves through a society that is rife with dissatisfaction and deep desire for a new order. The "good news" of Jesus was good only to those who were outside the power structures. To the hierarchy, Jesus was annoying, threatening, disrespectful, and dangerous. Regardless of what he might accomplish on his own, Jesus had great potential to incite the "rabble" to riot. At the very least, Jesus rippled the calm waters of the status quo.

Judaism at the time of Jesus was a well-established faith, even though it was subject to regulation by the Roman Empire. The leaders of the Jewish people had much invested in maintaining the religious organizational structures that supported them. It was inevitable that these leaders would stop at nothing to end the threat of anyone who challenged them. The commitment that the Jewish leaders had to institutional Judaism blinded them to the truths of Jesus the Christ. Even the Son of God was not exempt from the shortsightedness of the Pharisees, priests, and scribes. When Jesus came bearing a new message, the good news, few people at the top had ears to hear. Fortunately, many people, within Judaism and beyond, did hear; and they shared what they heard with others. The challenging new ideas of Jesus the Christ carried forth throughout the world, and the world was forever changed.

A Different Kind of Teaching

One of Jesus' primary teaching methods was the parable. Although parables were common teaching tools in the early first century, Jesus used them in a radically different way. A parable is a short story that contains an ironic twist or a complete absurdity intended to drive home a moral point or religious principle. It is designed so that the hearer will associate himself or herself with the subject of the opening sentence. Parables use nonreligious language and images to illustrate deep religious truths. Parables are puzzle language; the listener has to pay close attention and give serious thought to know what the parable means. Jesus was a master of teaching in parables, and he used parables often to challenge the established social order.

In Jesus' time, however, parables were not considered an appropriate medium for teaching important information. Parables and fables were used to teach children and to convey folk knowledge and proverbial truth. Most religious leaders in Jerusalem would have considered the parable a lesser form, well beneath the dignity of the Temple. Although most leaders knew many popular parables, few would lower themselves to use them. When Jesus of Nazareth came teaching in parables, it was one more reason for the religious hierarchy to hold him in contempt.

The religious leaders did not realize that the common people loved the provincial charm of this folk teaching, so the leaders ignored the impact that this teaching had. Suddenly, the people were learning the deep truths of their faith outside the confines of the Temple and synagogue. A new way of learning was offered; and it came not through the formal structures but from someone outside. In yet another significant way, Jesus proved to be a threat to the established order.

A Reflective Moment Along the Way

Since the beginning of time and creation of the world, God has continued to create. God is a "Living God" who chooses to move us into the future through change. Change, even through paradigm shifts, is God's way of leading us forward into a new reality called the kingdom of God.

Prepare for your group meeting by remembering a time when God led you to see a life situation or experience in a new way. How did it feel? What did you learn from the experience?

During your group meeting you may be asked to tell another person about this experience and your learning from it.

Key Concepts for the Journey
Paradigms

Once it was believed that the earth was flat, then it was proved to be round. Once the earth was believed to be at the center of the universe, then it was proved that the sun stands at the center of earth's orbit. Once it was believed that people of color were inferior to Caucasians, but no intelligent person believes that today. Once it was believed that women should not be ordained as ministers in The United Methodist Church, but today women provide excellent leadership that the church lacked for centuries. Times change, and the things that were "right" or "true" in the past are no longer "right" or "true." Each of these changes constitutes a "paradigm shift."

A paradigm is a set of assumptions, rules, opinions, and ideas that describes reality. What "is" is not as important as what is "understood to be." Paradigms are both the reality in which we find ourselves (macro) and the lenses through which we view reality (micro). We live in certain paradigms, and we live out of certain paradigms. Some paradigms cannot be denied, while others are hotly contested.

Ours is a technological age. Computers have redefined the way we live. Even for those who choose not to become "computer-literate," computers affect every aspect of their lives. A paradigm has shifted from a time when computers did not exist to a time when virtually nothing takes place that does not rely upon some form of computer technology.

A century ago, the "travel paradigm" looked quite different than it does today. Imagine life without automobiles, airplanes, buses, motorcycles, and the like. What if there were no highways, paved roadways, or interstates? Some might think this sounds nice, but few would choose to return to those days.

Think of the movement of information. In a century, we have added phone, fax, computer, television, wireless radio, satellite, telephone, magnetic and digital recording, microfilm, and dozens of other key inventions to the way information is created, transferred, stored, and retrieved. An Indiana billboard claims that in 1957, more than three million manual typewriters were sold in the United States. In 1997, fewer than one thousand were sold; and most of those were sold as antiques, not for use. It is possible to hold on to the old way of doing things when the paradigm shifts, but doing so will seriously impair a person's ability to keep up with the rest of the world.

Paradigms also shift within the church. Loren Mead discusses the shifting paradigms affecting the Christian church in *The Once and Future Church*. Mead identifies three main paradigm shifts that the church has experienced since the time of Jesus: the Apostolic paradigm, the Christendom paradigm, and a newly emerging, yet-to-be-defined paradigm.[1]

The Apostolic paradigm lasted through the time when Christianity moved from Jerusalem into the world. During that time, it was dangerous to be a Christian. Theology was in formation, and there was a continual battle to clarify orthodoxy from heresy. There was incredible energy in the church as people dedicated themselves to taking the good news to the ends of the earth. This era came to a close when the Christian church became institutionalized as the "state religion" of the Roman Empire in the fourth century. Thus began the Christendom era.

The age of Christendom began during the reign of Constantine and lasted well into the twentieth century. Christendom is characterized by the centrality of the Christian faith to the social, political, and family life of the dominant culture. In the Christendom paradigm, the church is central, and church leaders are revered and respected. Church teaching carries the weight of law. The church is the gathering place for people, not only on Sunday, but also throughout the week. People often identify themselves by their sect or creed. In short, the church is highly valued by the entire culture, even by those outside the institution. The popular view of the church is that of a good, holy, necessary institution that is central to the identity of a community. This perspective dominated for centuries.

Now in the twenty-first century a new paradigm is emerging—one that Mead claims is yet to be fully formed—that many label as the "post-Christendom paradigm." The church—and the leadership within the church—is no longer revered as it once was. People are much more ready to dispute the teachings of the church; and if the church disappoints people, they walk away. The church no longer holds a high priority for many people. Sunday is rarely held apart as a day of rest—or, more pointedly, as a holy Sabbath.

The Christian church is experiencing competition as never before. Not only is there a greater awareness of world religions due to our booming global consciousness, but each week new spiritualities emerge that offer "new" answers and ancient truths. In the United States, hundreds of applications a day are filed for "new church status" with the federal government. While "being spiritual" has never been more popular, "being Christian" has never been more suspect. Established Christian churches from mainline denominations are just beginning to question seriously what all these changes mean. What significance do these trends have, and how can the church respond in a faithful and meaningful way? How do we remain faithful to the gospel of Jesus Christ, while reaching out to serve a new generation of seekers?

Dr. Ezra Earl Jones, a former general secretary of the General Board of Discipleship of The United Methodist Church, describes a distinction between the model of church organization at the end of the Christendom paradigm and the model of church organization that is emerging. The former model sought to preserve the institution. That model treats the church as an "activity center," where programs are offered to connect individuals with the institution. The primary beneficiary in the activity-center model is the church, not the individual believer. Emphasis is placed on membership; giving of time, talent, and money; and attending worship. In Christendom, where the church exerted a central influence over society, these emphases were feasible. Now the paradigm is shifting. What worked in the past is no longer appropriate. The characteristics of the new paradigm move us from the "activity center" to "community." To avoid confusion with the community surrounding each local church, we will refer to the model for the new paradigm as the "faith-forming community."

Figure 1A shows the significant shifts in church focus, decision points for participation, requirements for participants, and understanding of who does ministry as the church moves from one paradigm to the other.

While the focus of the "activity center" was on the institutional church, the focus of the "faith-forming community" is on building relationships between people and Jesus Christ. These relationships are dependent not upon people agreeing to join a church at one point in life, but upon people agreeing to embark upon a journey that lasts a lifetime. The requirements for inclusion in the faith-forming community are not institutional but formational. In the faith-forming community, members practice the means of grace: prayer, fasting, study of Scripture, attendance at the Lord's Supper, Christian conferencing (regular conversation with other Christians about faith development and growth), and the performance of acts of mercy and kindness both within and beyond the faith-forming community. No longer is faith protected as "personal and private"; but in the biblical and historical tradition of Christianity, faith is communal and accountable. As the institution recedes in importance, the professional staff gives way to the need for every member of the faith-forming community to be engaged in meaningful ministry. These changes will enable the church to respond to the paradigm shifts that have occurred in the world. What was appropriate in the past can no longer define the church of today and tomorrow. The paradigm has shifted. Only by shifting our own paradigms—creating new models for organization and ministry—will we be able to move forward through the twenty-first century.

It is important to remember that Jesus was a paradigm shifter. Jesus burst upon a religious world that wasn't ready to change, and the resistance he encountered caused his message to be taken to the Gentiles. Jesus offered many new ways to respond to the newly emerging paradigm of his day. Those who had ears to hear and those who had eyes to see made changes. Those blinded by the old ways lost out. To ignore paradigm shifts results in being left behind as the reality changes. It is only by learning to ride with the shift that we can hope to master the new paradigm and to grow stronger.

Resistance to Change

Change is disruptive. It may also be uncomfortable and unpleasant. Even necessary change is hard. The truth, though, is that change is inevitable. Each person has a crucial decision to make: "Will I change gracefully, or will I change kicking and screaming?"

Change is not really the problem, however. People don't mind changing; they mind *being changed*. When people feel a measure of control over what is happening to them, they can deal with change more gracefully. When people are forced to change, they are more likely to resist.

Paradigm shifts force people to change. After the electric light bulb became standard, few people held on to kerosene and candles. Once television became widespread, radio changed dramatically. The "family altar" shifted from the illuminated dial to the flickering screen. Super 8 film yielded to videotape, typewriters to word processors, slide rules to pocket calculators, and on and on. Even though there is some initial resistance to new technologies, most people soon assimilate them into their lifestyles; and then they grow dependent upon them—to the extent that they resist the next level of technological advancement.

New Information

New ideas and information are a form of change, and they are central to new and emerging paradigms. Whenever we receive new information, we have to do something with it. We either integrate it into our worldview, ignore it, or refute it. Rarely will we be unaffected by new information. Television has done much to change our understanding of the world and our place in it. Newspapers, magazines, and radio inundate us with information. We have more data at our disposal than ever before. Our children will forget more information by the time they leave middle school than we learned through four years of college. It is a challenge to feel "in control" of our lives when we are receiving new data by the minute. What we knew for a fact yesterday may no longer be relevant or true. For many, this is an insecure time to be alive.

The positive side is that information is power, and we are living in an information age. The para-

Figure 1A

THE CHURCH AS ACTIVITY CENTER		THE CHURCH AS FAITH-FORMING COMMUNITY
The Church	**FOCUS**	Jesus, the Christ
Initial Assent	**DECISION**	Journey
Commitment of Time, Talent, and Money	**REQUIREMENTS**	Practice of the Spiritual Disciplines
Individual	**ACCOUNTABILITY**	Small Group
Professional Staff	**MINISTRY**	All People

digm shift to an information-based world certainly tests our abilities to adapt and change, but it has enormous potential to make life better for everyone. Those who are able to master the information paradigm will succeed in the world ahead. As long as we view new information and new realities as possibilities for growth rather than as threats to the status quo, we should do just fine.

The church receives new information just as everyone else does. Church leaders face the same decisions about what to do with the information. For too long, many church leaders have opted to ignore the new information, pretending that it has nothing to do with them. They have ignored cultural and generational trends. The church often adopts the attitude that newcomers will be won over to the church's way of seeing things. The fact that younger people and many people of other cultures don't support highly organized institutional structures is viewed as their problem, not the church's. When these same people seek Christian community elsewhere, some church leaders shake their heads and wonder, "What's wrong with them?" Ignoring new information is one of the quickest paths out of existence.

Another popular position within the church has been to refute new information. One denominational official, when confronted with statistics of precipitous membership and attendance declines in his church, said that the declines were actually a good thing because they proved that people were being challenged. He stated that the real problem with the church was all the fault-finders who were looking for trouble when there really wasn't any. Adoption of an "us-against-them" mentality won't help the church through times of transition. Arguing about the shifting reality does little to address change productively. The church cannot afford to waste time debating the nature of the change when lives and souls are at stake. The church needs to integrate new information into its worldview.

Information about changing trends in education, business, religion, politics, family, societal morality, technology, and a thousand other topics affects our daily lives. Anything that affects the lives of the people in the church is important information for church leaders. We do not serve the needs of the people who come to our churches if we ignore or argue with the changing realities of their lives. Jesus offers us a model for dealing with the shifting paradigms of life. He knew the hearts and minds of the people he served, taught, and healed. He listened carefully, and he met people where they were in their lives and faith development. At no time did Jesus ever compromise the mission and message he was sent to proclaim; but he was ever attentive to the needs, wants, hopes, and hurts of the people. This is what is needed in our day. This is what it means to be the church.

The world is changing. We are living in a new age, a new church paradigm. How can we be faithful? The best way is to focus our attention on the one with the power to rebuke the wind and calm the waves—Jesus Christ, the shifter of paradigms and the bearer of a new way of thinking and living. As leaders in the church, we serve best in changing times by anchoring ourselves to the Christ who makes all things new.

Questions for Discussion

Jesus offered a number of challenges to the paradigms of his day. Reflect upon the teachings of the Sermon on the Plain in Luke 6:20-26. How would you react if tomorrow morning the realities of the rich and poor, the hungry and well-fed, and the joyful and sorrowful were reversed? Where would you find yourself? What does this passage teach you about God and Jesus Christ?

What personal paradigm shifts have you experienced? What cultural paradigm shifts? What church paradigm shifts?

When the paradigms shift and change occurs, which response best characterizes your congregation?
   (a) We grow nostalgic for the past.
   (b) We recite the words "We've never done it that way before!"
   (c) We keep on doing what we've been doing.
   (d) We seek new programs, ideas, and resources to address changing needs.
   (e) We work together to figure out the best way to serve the greatest number of needs of the greatest number of people.

When is change easiest in your congregation? When is it most difficult?

Who is most often responsible for change within your congregation?

_____

_____

_____

_____

_____

Discovery
Naming Our Current Reality: Paradigms

Understanding the paradigms that exist around us helps us understand our current reality. Current reality is the way we describe who we are, where we are, and what we are doing. Sometimes we have difficulty seeing our current reality because we are too close to it. When we step back to look at the changing paradigms all around us and ask ourselves how we are responding to these changes, we are often surprised to find that we are out of step. This is a prevalent message in our day: the church is out of step with the rest of the world.

The cultural paradigm has shifted from Christendom to post-Christendom. The appropriate church paradigm for the post-Christendom world bears little resemblance to the church paradigm during Christendom. We need a new organizational model to move us from the "church as activity-center" paradigm to the "church as faith-forming-community" paradigm.

Examine the two lists in Figure 1B. The list on the left, labeled "Activity Center," reflects the model of most churches—in the activity-center paradigm. The list on the right, labeled "Faith-Forming Community," names the elements that are essential for creating faith-forming community. When so much energy is used to maintain the "busy-ness" of the activity-centered church, there is little or no time for the spiritual disciplines that bond people together in a life-transforming way. What needs to change in a congregation to move it from the activity-center model to the faith-forming-community model? What immediate changes might a church experience if it stopped doing the things on the left? What immediate changes might a church experience if it gave more time to practicing the means of grace listed on the right?

What holds our church in place and prevents us from creating a faith-forming community? What will move us toward the faith-forming community?

What evidence supports the argument that the activity-center model is no longer working? What evidence suggests that there is need for the faith-forming-community model?

What are the challenges to designing a faith-forming community?

_____

_____

_____

_____

_____

_____

Change

Change has a natural "life cycle," illustrated in the shaded area of Figure 1C. If the life cycle is disrupted, then the chance for successful change is diminished. Once a person perceives the need for change, he or she should communicate that perception. Awareness of the need for change is critical. The more people there are who are aware of the need for a change, the more support there will be.

When someone identifies a necessary change, listen to all the opinions about how to change. Talk about all the options. Help create understanding about how various changes will meet the need. Once there is clarity about the best path to follow, you will be able to develop a design to implement the change. Then you can test, evaluate, and accept or reject the change.

Unfortunately, we often try to find shortcuts in this life cycle. Many times, after a need for change has been identified, the task of implementing the change is handed to a small group, task force, or committee. Group members work to the best of their

Session 1: A New Paradigm

ACTIVITY CENTER	FAITH-FORMING COMMUNITY
Christian Education Committee	Prayer
Membership Work Area	Lord's Supper
Stewardship Committee	Study of Scripture
Worship Committee	Acts of Mercy
Evangelism Committee	Christian Conference
Church and Society Committee	Fasting and Abstinence
Missions Work Area	

Figure 1B

abilities—with the best interests of the congregation in mind. Then they come back to "try something out" on the church. More often than not, the new idea is summarily rejected, which causes hurt feelings and makes further changes even more difficult.

An illustration of this comes from two churches with a similar "positive" problem: too many people in worship caused everyone to feel cramped. Both churches perceived a need for more space. Both decided that they wanted to expand the seating capacity of their sanctuaries. One understood the life cycle of change and the importance of conversation. That congregation called a small group together to survey the congregation about the need for more space. One of the earliest plans for discussion was the addition of a balcony. As this option was shared, many people reacted with horror that the beauty of the sanctuary would be compromised and that the balcony would make those in the rear of the sanctuary feel claustrophobic. Money concerns were also raised. A number of people suggested having multiple services. As more people got involved in the discussion, it became clear that the idea of an alternative service with a different style of music and preaching was very popular. The church could grow, more people could worship, the congregation would reach out to different needs in the community, and the existing sanctuary would remain intact. Many people took part in planning and designing the new service; and it was tested—to rave reviews. The new service eased the crowding because it drew some of the

Figure 1C

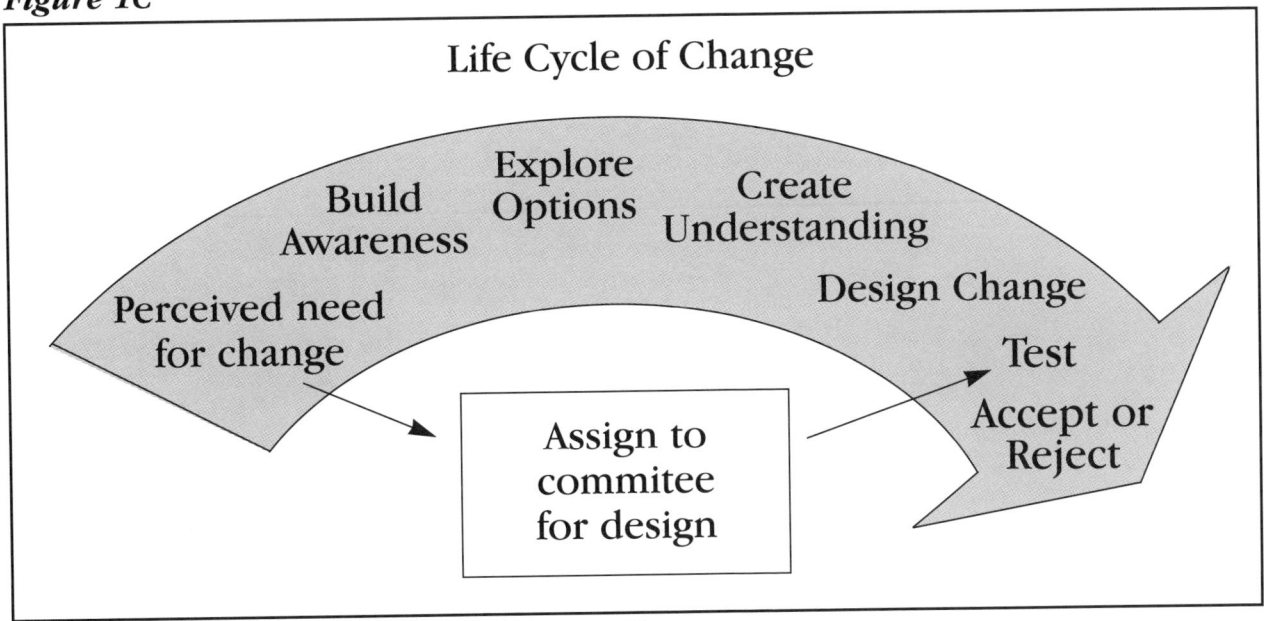

Life Cycle of Change

Perceived need for change → Build Awareness → Explore Options → Create Understanding → Design Change → Test → Accept or Reject

Assign to commitee for design

17

overflow from the more traditional service. In time, the church grew by such numbers that it needed to expand the sanctuary, and money was no longer a concern.

The other church disrupted the life cycle of change as illustrated under the shaded area of Figure 1C. That congregation authorized the trustees to investigate the costs of adding one hundred seats to the sanctuary. The trustees reported that the extra space could be obtained by adding a balcony at the rear of the historic sanctuary. Some funds were available through a building endowment fund. Very little information was shared with the congregation until the plans were unveiled. During the summer months, the congregation worshiped with their Presbyterian neighbors while construction took place. With grumbling and misgivings expressed, the church forged ahead and built the balcony. When it was completed, almost everyone agreed that the balcony ruined the charm of the sanctuary, that the sound and lighting under the balcony were inadequate, and that the balcony itself "didn't feel safe." Some people stayed away, and a few even changed churches. Within months, the numbers dwindled to the extent that the extra seating wasn't even required.

In what ways is your congregation effective at building awareness, exploring options, and creating understanding when change is required or inevitable? In what ways do you shortcut the life cycle of change?

For Resources, Teaching Aids, and Newest Information

Check out our website at www.faithquest.net. There you will find additional information about the biblical concepts of Session 1. You will also find book reviews, movie reviews, and guidance for your spiritual life.

SESSION 2:
Understanding God's Purpose

Scriptures:
- Luke 9:51–17:37; 24:44-49
- Matthew 28:18-20
  Focus Verses: Luke 10:1-12, 17-20

Key Biblical Concepts:
- Discipleship
- Jesus defines the mission of the church
- Jesus challenges the leadership of the day
- Jesus teaches people how to relate to one another

Key Concepts for the Journey:
- Mission
- Vision
- Aim

Outline:
- Gathering
- A Time of Centering
- Prayer
- Preparation
  Questions and Answers
- Exploration
  A Reflective Moment Along the Way
  Questions and Small-Group Exercises
- Discovery
- Conclusion

Introduction

What is the mission of the church? What does God expect from us? How can we faithfully serve and honor God in all we say and do?

Jesus was clear in redefining what it meant to be the people of God. The Gospel of Luke shows the variety of ways that people received the call of God to be the church. This session will explore the mission of the church for our day and the way we can catch a vision for ministry.

Prayer

Gracious and loving God, teach us to pray as Jesus did in the garden: "not my will be done, but thine." Give us a vision for ministry and a clarity of our call to serve faithfully within the body of Christ. Make us receptive to opportunities to serve and save and love. Grant us your power, your grace, and your courage to be faithful disciples in our world today. Amen.

Preparation
Daily Scripture References and Questions for Reflection

Day 1 — Luke 9:51–10:42

What is the mission of the seventy as defined by Jesus? How does the parable of the good Samaritan expand the mission?

_____
_____
_____
_____
_____
_____

19

Day 2 — Luke 11:1–12:48

How does Jesus' teaching about prayer inform our understanding of God? In these passages, what teachings about faith, trust, and obedience do you find? Spend some time today praying as God leads you for the other participants beginning this FaithQuest study with you.

Day 3 — Luke 12:49–14:35

What hard (personally challenging) messages do you encounter in these passages?

Day 4 — Luke 15:1-32

What "visions" emerge from these three parables? How do they align with the mission Jesus defined for the disciples?

Day 5 — Luke 16:1–17:37

How does Jesus address people's relationships with money and with other people? What do these passages tell us about God?

Day 6 — Matthew 28:18-20, Luke 24:44-49

Compare and contrast Jesus' parting instructions in these two passages. How would you state the mission of the church, using these two passages and the mission of the seventy as defined in Luke 10?

Also read the session material and make notes in the margins.

Exploration
Background Information: The Journey to Jerusalem and Beyond

In the fifty-first verse of the ninth chapter of Luke, the author writes that Jesus "set his face to go to Jerusalem." A better way of understanding this passage would be to say that Jesus set every fiber of his being to the task that was before him. He clearly focused on his mission in life: to rendezvous with the cross of Calvary.

This is, perhaps, one of the most significant passages in the entire gospel. It is the turning point of

Luke's gospel, and every event from this passage forward throughout both Luke and Acts hinges upon it. It is at this point in the gospel that the mission of the church comes into focus. Jesus sends seventy disciples into the world to proclaim the arrival of the kingdom of God. Repentance and forgiveness are the cornerstones of the Kingdom. The empowerment of the Holy Spirit drives the mission of the church. It is at this point that the followers of Jesus Christ are given their marching orders. The first order is to spread the good news among the people of Israel and Judea. But there is more, as Jesus encourages his followers to proclaim the good news to the ends of the earth. The account written in the Book of Acts carries the message beyond the Jewish community to the entire known world. Jesus is establishing a new paradigm: forgiveness and acceptance for all the world!

The image of the journey is strong throughout Luke and Acts. In Luke, Jesus is on the move; and wherever he goes, amazing things happen. It is important to note that Jesus never saw planting and establishing churches as part of his mission. His mission was to connect all people to the kingdom of God. The church existed for Jesus wherever two or more gathered to honor and praise God. The church was never stationary but was always on the move, reaching out to new people in new places.

Prayer

Another central image in the Gospel of Luke is that of Jesus in prayer. Prayer is a primary work of the church. It provides a strong foundation for the work that needs to be done, and it connects the one who ministers to God. It refocuses the one who serves on the true mission of the church. Repeatedly, the work of Jesus is either preceded or followed by a time of intensive prayer. Jesus instructs the disciples in prayer in the eleventh chapter of Luke, and he promises that the Holy Spirit will provide for their every need. Throughout his life, Jesus modeled the critical importance of prayer.

Discipleship

What does it mean to be a disciple of Jesus Christ? Does it mean to believe that Jesus is the Son of God? Does that make a person a disciple? Or does being a disciple mean ordering one's life after the teaching and example of Jesus? Does it mean to do and say the things that Jesus did and said? Does being a member of a church make a person a disciple? Is discipleship the ultimate goal of Christian faith?

Luke's definition of a Christian disciple might be a little bit different from what we expect. Disciples were students, followers, and apprentices. They were "in training." Discipleship was a phase of Christian development. Being a disciple was much like being a "rookie" today. Jesus had high expectations that his followers would leave behind their discipleship for a life of active Christian service.

The visitation of the Holy Spirit at Pentecost in Acts 2 is a significant event on many levels. Perhaps the most overlooked significance has to do with the "graduation" of the Twelve. Until the Pentecost event, the Twelve are referred to as "disciples." After Pentecost, they are never referred to as disciples again, only as "apostles." At this point, the only people referred to as disciples in Scripture are the followers of the apostles. At some point, disciples experience a transformation in the Holy Spirit that moves them to a new phase of Christian service. The relationship between the Christian and the Christ deepens.

In the Gospel of Matthew, Jesus offers the Great Commission: "All authority in heaven and on earth has been given to me. Go therefore and make disciples of all nations, baptizing them in the name of the Father and of the Son and of the Holy Spirit, and teaching them to obey everything that I have commanded you. And remember, I am with you always, to the end of the age" (Matthew 28:18-20). This, seemingly, defines the fundamental work of the church as the making of disciples. But the questions remain, "What do you do with a bunch of disciples?" "What is the purpose of a disciple?"

The parting words of Jesus in the Gospel of Luke, what some have referred to as the "Greater Commission," help give perspective to the disciple questions. In Luke 24:47-49, Jesus says that "repentance and forgiveness of sins is to be proclaimed in [the Messiah's] name to all nations, beginning from Jerusalem. You are witnesses of these things. And see, I am sending upon you what my Father promised; so stay here in the city until you have been clothed with power from on high." When these passages are brought together, it becomes clear that the work of discipleship is to proclaim repentance and forgiveness to all nations in the power of the Holy Spirit so that the kingdom of God might finally be realized upon the earth. This mission and the vision of a global kingdom of God is the motivating image that John Wesley used to birth Methodism. This mission provided the fertile soil from which mighty visions for ministry emerged that established the Christian church in the world for all time.

A Reflective Moment Along the Way

Reread the words from Luke 24:47-49. As part of this "Greater Commission," Jesus tells his disciples to "stay here in the city until you have been clothed with power from on high." He knew that the Holy Spirit would empower his followers to share the mission to the "ends of the earth."

Many people find it difficult to share Jesus' new way to understand life. When have you felt empowered "from on high" to share your faith with someone? Who first told you about God? Does your church help people discover nonthreatening ways to talk about God? What are those ways? If not, what could be done? Be prepared to talk about responses to these questions when you meet with your FaithQuest group.

Key Concepts for the Journey
Mission

The mission of an organization answers the question "What business are we in?" The mission is our reason for being. It clearly communicates why we exist and what we plan to accomplish. Any organization that is not clear about its mission will not be effective, and it may not survive.

The Christian church has long debated its mission. Some say that the mission of the church is to make disciples of Jesus Christ. Others say the church exists to serve the poor and marginalized. Some believe that the church exists to spread holiness across the land. Some say that the church exists to challenge the dark forces at work in the world. Time spent in defining the mission takes time away from accomplishing the mission. **Figuring out the one right mission for an organization is not as important as agreeing upon a mission that motivates people to give their best effort to make it happen.** As long as the mission of an organization reflects the core shared values of the organization's members and clearly serves a needed purpose, then that mission will enable the organization to be effective. Reading the four gospels, it is possible to arrive at any of a dozen reasonable definitions of the mission of the Christian church. One is no more "right" than any other. What is most important is clearly stating a mission and aligning all human and material resources to serve that mission faithfully.

In 1996, the General Conference of The United Methodist Church clearly stated a mission for the denomination: "to make disciples of Jesus Christ." United Methodism has chosen to focus on Matthew 28:19-20 as the source of its missional definition. Numerous groups and individuals argue that this is not an adequate mission for the church. Alternatives have been debated, but to no productive end. Making disciples is a good and worthy mission as long as we have a clear sense about *why* we are making disciples. This mission of making disciples gives The United Methodist Church a position from which it may serve in the world. What disciple-making looks like and the impact it will have on the world will vary from place to place. But with clarity of mission, all churches can align their resources to fulfill their disciple-making role faithfully.

Vision

When you think of the mission "to make disciples of Jesus Christ," what images come to mind? What does a disciple look like? How would the world benefit if we were successful at making disciples? How would the creation of disciples honor and glorify God? These pictures, or images, are a vision of what fulfillment of the mission might be. Pictures motivate people to act. When we can see something, we can strive to create it—to transform an idea into reality.

One impressive story of vision concerns a woman named Mona Ball from St. Louis, Missouri. Mona was the daughter of a successful financier, the widow of an investment banker, and a respected insurance adjuster on her own. At age fifty-seven, she was immensely wealthy; but she felt her life was missing something. As she recounts the story, it occurred to her that in fifty-seven years she could not recall ever once committing a charitable act. Everything she had done had been for her personal gain. She wondered what she could do that would make a significant difference. When she was fifty-nine, she suffered a long-term illness that left her unable to return to work. Daily, she sat by the bay window of her brownstone in the heart of the St. Louis financial district. Each day at noon, Mona watched as the city's indigent gathered on the street corners to beg from business people on their lunch breaks. After a week or so, Mona saw a strange sight. One particular afternoon, as Mona pulled back her curtains, she was struck by the image of dozens of St. Louis street people eating sandwiches and drinking coffee. She blinked her eyes and looked again, but this time the street people were milling around as usual, begging for whatever change they could get. For days, the vision of the people eating and drinking haunted her. As she considered the vision, she thought, "I could do that." The thought surprised her; but as she reflected, she realized that she could provide a simple lunch to the few people who gathered on the street corner. The next day at noon, Mona appeared on the steps of her brownstone with a tray of sandwiches and a thermos of coffee.

In the weeks that followed, word spread of Mona Ball's kindness. Hundreds of people from all over the city gathered for lunch. Mona wondered how she would be able to provide enough food for the growing crowd. One day, as she stepped outside to distribute sandwiches, she was amazed to see another door open down the street; a second woman emerged with a second tray of sandwiches. In the ensuing months, more and more people pitched in to feed more and more people. Today, thousands of lunches are provided each month at the Ball Mission. This work began through a simple vision to feed the hungry.

Vision has the power to transform lives. When people are caught up in the power of vision, they will accomplish incredible things. Repeatedly, Jesus offered visions of what the world could be, what people could accomplish, and what the rewards would be for faithfulness to God. These visions were compelling, and they enabled ordinary people to achieve extraordinary results.

It is difficult to accomplish great things without powerful vision. Vision acts as a magnet, drawing us toward the achievement of our mission. When the picture is attractive, people are naturally drawn to it. Unfortunately, many churches have no clear vision for ministry. Leaders of congregations sometimes lack a picture of how they might fulfill their mission. The sharing of vision within a Christian community is essential for growth and faithful discipleship.

Aim

Mission plus vision equals aim. When there is clarity about mission, when there is a vision for effectively accomplishing that mission, then a specific aim appears. The aim answers the question "What are you trying to accomplish?" Figure 2A shows how focusing on mission leads to vision. Mission plus vision provides the direction, or aim, for action.

It is interesting to note how few church leaders can answer the question "What is your church trying to accomplish?" Several leaders from one congregation may offer a variety of answers. When this happens, it usually means that there is not a clearly understood mission or a shared vision for ministry. Unless the mission and vision are widely understood, it is highly unlikely that the members of a congregation will share the same aim.

One word of caution: *Mission* and *vision* have become cultural buzzwords—words reduced in meaning by overuse and misunderstanding. Organizations today spend a great deal of time and effort developing mission and vision statements. Unfortunately, such exercises miss the point of mission and vision.

A mission is a reason for being. If people in an organization do not know why the organization exists, they may be in the wrong place. A mission statement doesn't need to be written. It should be a part of the heart and mind of every member of the organization. If it cannot be remembered without being written, it is not worth remembering. If a mission is worthy, no one will be able to forget it.

As a simple exercise, ask members of your group to state the mission of your church without looking it up. When you gather with leaders of other congregations, ask them to recite the mission statements of their churches. Don't be embarrassed if you can't articulate your church's mission—or surprised when

AIM IS MISSION PLUS VISION

Mission | Vision

Aim

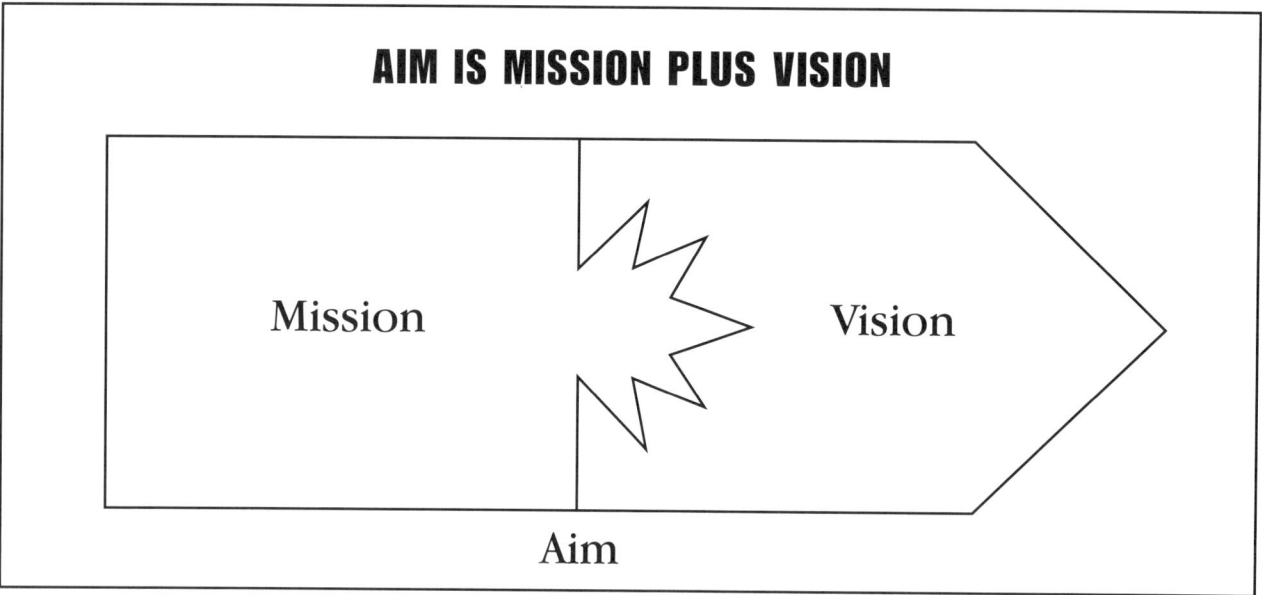

Figure 2A

others can't. Few people can. We have taken a fundamental identity process (articulating the mission) and have turned it into a writing assignment. We should be discussing the importance of the mission, not wrestling with the "right" words to print on a page.

What is true of mission is even more true of vision. A vision is something you see, not something you read or hear. Vision is fluid and evolving. Vision is not fixed like a photograph; it moves like an image on film. When we write a vision statement, we create a snapshot, not a living image. Further, vision is subjective. Many people might view one particular scene and come away with very different opinions about what they saw. It is in the exchange and interplay of different visions that creativity and alternatives appear. Vision is a synergistic process, where the end result is always greater than the sum of the parts. One person might have a compelling vision; however, it is through the addition of many different perspectives on this vision that shared vision is created.

Writing a vision statement limits the possibilities and impedes creativity. Continuously sharing vision and lifting new ideas and opinions regularly infuses an organization with new energy. Mission usually doesn't change much. Since mission reflects the core values and principles of an organization, it remains fairly constant. Vision changes regularly, and it reflects the changing needs of the community that the organization serves. Even though mission and vision are different, they are tied together to define the work of the organization. They also share another important attribute: both are significantly limited when they are reduced to paper.

Continue to reflect on your mission. Regularly discuss your vision. Never write them down, or you may end up somewhere you really don't want to be.

Questions for Discussion

How do the members of the congregation understand the mission of the church? In what ways do you communicate the mission clearly and regularly?

What is the vision of your congregation? What compelling pictures draw you into the future?

How is your understanding of mission and vision affected by the shift from an activity-center paradigm to a faith-forming-community paradigm?

Be prepared to discuss these questions with others when your FaithQuest group meets.

Discovery
Naming Our Current Reality

It is important for United Methodist congregations to discuss the implications of the mission adopted by the 1996 General Conference. If our mission is to make disciples of Jesus Christ, what does this mean? How do we go about this task? How do we best use our human and material resources to make disciples? The relationship of mission and vision is illustrated in Figure 2B. The mission is like the frame around a television screen—it defines the boundaries and provides a context. Vision is the picture within that frame—always changing, with new images constantly emerging, but always bound by the context of the mission. What is our vision for making disciples?

Exercise

Alfred B. Nobel, the great inventor, awoke one morning to read his own obituary in the newspaper. In actuality, his brother had passed away, but the newspaper had mistakenly run Alfred Nobel's obituary instead of his brother's. What Nobel read distressed and disheartened him. Nobel, at this point in his life, was best known as the inventor of dynamite. The obituary credited him with the creation of the most destructive force then known to humankind. Dynamite was just being introduced by the military as a weapon, and the article speculated about the kind of death and devastation that dynamite could create. As Nobel read these words of remembrance, he asked himself, "Is this what I want to be known for?" Through this ironic twist of fate, Nobel was able to see himself in a way few people ever do. On that day, he committed his life to the building up of humanity, rather than to its destruction. He pledged that he would be known for his good works; and in his will he established the Nobel prizes for the humanities.[2] Now, Nobel is known worldwide as a man of peace, a man of science and letters, a great humanitarian. He became a man in pursuit of a strong personal vision.

Personal vision provides the motivation to accomplish specific goals and to fulfill a sense of purpose. Upon your death in the far distant future, how would you like to be remembered? What changes do you need to make in your life to achieve your goals? What would you like to accomplish within the next two years? Five years? Ten years?

Part of vision is visualization: seeing what you want to have happen. A famous experiment involved three sets of people who were selected to shoot free throws with a basketball. All three groups shot ten free throws each, and the results were recorded. The first group was told to practice shooting free throws for twenty minutes each day for a month. The second group was instructed to do nothing—no practice, no thinking about shooting free throws, nothing. The last group was asked to spend twenty minutes a day visualizing shooting and making free throws. All they had to do was shoot free throws in their minds. At the end of the month, the three groups were tested. Group one showed a forty-three percent improvement in making free-throw shots. Group two showed virtually no change. Group three, however, improved by a rate of forty-two percent, almost as much as the first group. Visualization—as seen in this experiment—improves performance and moves people toward their goals.

As we learn to visualize the accomplishment of life goals, we find that we are moving in that direction. Without vision, we are adrift, and it is difficult to move in a positive direction. Life just happens to us. With vision, we take hold of life and make the most of every opportunity.

A shared vision for our church is also important. What do we want for our church? How can we fulfill the church's mission in combination with other men and women who have their own visions for ministry? The apostle Paul refers to the "body" as a metaphor for the church. In what ways is the church

Figure 2B

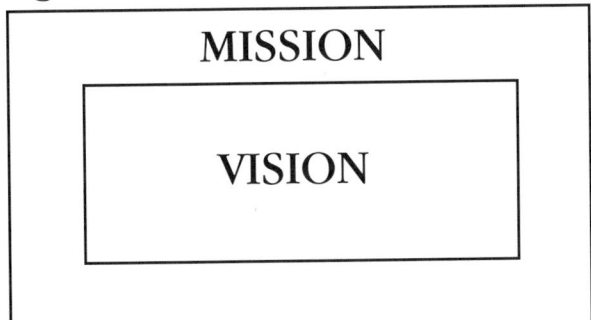

```
┌─────────────────────────────────┐
│           MISSION               │
│   ┌─────────────────────────┐   │
│   │                         │   │
│   │        VISION           │   │
│   │                         │   │
│   └─────────────────────────┘   │
│                                 │
└─────────────────────────────────┘
```

like a body? How are the individual members of the body joined? As you visualize the church as a body, where do you see yourself? Are you clear about where other individuals fit? Prepare to talk with your group about the images that come to your mind.

For Resources, Teaching Aids, and Newest Information

Check out our website at www.faithquest.net.

SESSION 3:
Doing God's Will

Scriptures:
- Luke 9:10-17; 18:18–21:38
  Focus Verses: Luke 9:10-17

Key Biblical Concepts:
- Jesus established clear procedures for ministry
- Jesus redefined the rules for appropriate conduct
- Jesus kept a clear vision of "the big picture"

Key Concepts for the Journey:
- Processes
- Systems
- Organizational structures
- Optimization and suboptimization

Outline:
- Gathering
- A Time of Centering
- Prayer
- Preparation
  Questions and Answers
- Exploration
  A Reflective Moment Along the Way
  Questions and Small-Group Exercises
- Discovery
- Conclusion

Introduction

Jesus not only defined the mission of the church and called disciples to do the work, he also trained the disciples in the proper way to do the work. Jesus modeled a systematic approach to ministry, and he developed structures that the disciples could follow. Jesus involved the disciples in the work of Kingdom-building by giving them a clear objective, tools and resources to use, and concise instructions to follow. His leadership is a valuable model for the church in our day.

Prayer

Almighty God, give us insight to be able to use our gifts and talents in the best possible way. As faithful stewards, teach us to work smarter rather than harder so that we might maximize our potential to honor and glorify you and to serve you faithfully in the name of Jesus Christ our Lord. Amen.

Preparation
Daily Scripture References and Questions for Reflection

Day 1— Luke 9:10-17

How would you describe the process for feeding the five thousand? Who participated in making the miracle happen?

_____
_____
_____
_____
_____
_____

Day 2 — Luke 18:18–19:27

Jesus is systematic in his teachings. Describe the process Jesus uses in dealing with the rich young ruler (Luke 18:18-30). In the parable of the talents (Luke 19:11-27), what is Jesus teaching about the way we should live in the world?

Day 3 — Luke 19:28-48
What do you think Jesus experienced as he entered Jerusalem for the last time? Did knowing that he faced crucifixion make his entrance more difficult?

Day 4 — Luke 20:1-47
Who does Jesus challenge in the last week of his life? What does Jesus say about the existing system of leadership?

Day 5 — Luke 21:1-38
What is Jesus' vision of the present and of the future in Luke 21?

Day 6
Read the session material and make notes in the margins.

Exploration
Background Information: An Urgent Message for an Urgent Time

We may find it difficult today to grasp fully the urgency and intensity of the Gospel of Luke. The Jesus of the Gospel of Luke is on an important mission, with only a short time to fulfill it. He has three short years to create a lasting system upon which the kingdom of God can be built; three years to teach and train and prepare a small group of men and women to move forward throughout the world to create a whole new social order; three years to rock the foundations of one of the oldest and most enduring religious structures in history; three years to redefine God and God's relationship to all people. When we contemplate Jesus as he is entering Jerusalem and preparing to meet his destiny on the cross, it is easy for us to speculate that Jesus may have had some misgivings about whether or not everything was ready for his departure. His teachings have a sense of urgency, and he emphasizes being watchful, alert, and prepared.

This is a time of serious instruction for the disciples. In the few remaining days, Jesus reminds the disciples of the many key teachings of the ministry. Jesus urges the disciples to remain faithful and hopeful through the trials to come.

In this last period together, Jesus reemphasizes

his commitment to the needs of the poor, the lost, the outcast, and the marginalized. Jesus addresses the issues of wealth, poverty, and faithfulness. He deals with lepers, children, and widows. Nowhere is Jesus' concern for the poor and marginalized more evident than in Luke's account. The church exists to serve, and no one is more worthy of service than the least of the children of God.

There is no time to wait. Jesus ushered in the kingdom of God. Kingdom time is now. There is no need to wait for the return of the Christ. People need the good news today. People are losing their lives and their souls. Discipleship places a claim on our lives. Our service begins immediately and lasts a lifetime. Jesus underscores the urgency of the need to be ready and active throughout these passages of Scripture.

Jesus As Systematic Leader

It is appropriate to examine the way Jesus teaches and performs healings and miracles. At a casual glance, the stories in the gospels seem random and unrelated. Jesus moves from place to place; and everywhere he goes, he teaches, heals, and performs miracles. But the random appearance is deceiving. Jesus follows formulaic processes repeatedly throughout the gospels. It is impressive to see the precision with which Jesus works. When Jesus teaches, he uses set formats. The Sermon on the Mount in Matthew and the similar Sermon on the Plain in Luke begin with blessings and move to a detailed explanation of rules of conduct and practices of the day. When Jesus teaches in parables, he follows a set formula for parables, never deviating from it. Jesus often heals by first asking a question of the audience, then proceeding to perform a miracle. In the feeding of the five thousand, there is a very specific system in place. Jesus instructs the disciples to gather the crowd into groups of fifty. He then blesses and breaks the loaves and fish and hands them off to the disciples. The disciples, in turn, move through the crowd, breaking the loaves and fish; then they move on. Members within the groups continue the process by breaking bread and fish for one another. The miracle continues through the ranks, with many people participating. The outcome is that everyone is fed, and food is left for the journey home. Jesus tells the disciples to give the crowd food to eat; then he provides everything needed for the miracle to occur.

In story after story, there are clear objectives, tools, resources, and instructions for performance of the work; and others are involved who make the work happen. Even when Jesus heals a single individual, he includes the individual in the process by proclaiming, "Your faith has made you well." The gospel accounts are filled with processes and systems for the performance of the mission and ministry of the church.

A Reflective Moment Along the Way

For some people, talking about systems and processes sounds like "business talk." They wonder how it relates to the church's life. Jesus understood that life is a spiritual journey. In fact, he modeled that journey image by constantly moving from place to place and eventually to Jerusalem and Calvary's hill.

A journey is in reality a system consisting of many processes—life encounters and experiences of relationship with God and with others impact what we believe, what we do, and who we become as human beings.

Spend a few minutes thinking about your life journey. On a sheet of paper, list significant events, people, and experiences. Can you see how significant moments in your life have formed who you are today? Are you surprised at how many "processes" influenced your journey so far? The way processes are linked together is illustrated in Figure 3A. Be prepared to briefly talk about your insights when the FaithQuest group meets.

Key Concepts for the Journey
Processes

The alarm clock rings at 6:00 A.M. You stumble from bed, check the damage in the bathroom mirror, brush teeth, shower, shave, brush hair, dress, eat breakfast, and head for the door. By 7:00 A.M., you have already performed more than a dozen different processes, and the day has hardly begun.

There is a process to brushing teeth or showering or making and eating breakfast. The process may be different for each individual, but there is a process.

A process is defined simply as inputs, throughputs, and outputs that yield a specific outcome. The process of brushing teeth requires a brush, toothpaste, water, an open mouth with teeth in it, and a hand to make the toothbrush go (or hold the brush in place if it's electric). These are the inputs. The throughput is the combination of these things in a transformation process: the actual brushing of the teeth. As brush, paste, water, teeth, and hand work together, a change takes place. Outputs include a rinsed toothbrush, a rinsed mouth, a toweled-off chin, and a clean, fresh taste in the mouth. Taken together, this process of inputs, throughputs, and outputs yields the outcome of dental hygiene (you might want to floss as well, but that's another process).

Systems

Life is full of processes. When series of processes are aligned to accomplish a common aim, the result is a system. Systems are collections of processes. There are organic systems like the human body that involve thousands of interdependent processes. There are mechanistic systems like motors that involve either few or many processes. All systems are designed to realize a specific outcome. Each process in a system is important because it moves the larger system toward the desired outcome.

The church is also a system designed to fulfill a mission. Since its mission is making disciples, The United Methodist Church can be described as a disciple-making system. Each local church is a subsystem of the larger system of the annual conference. Each annual conference is a subsystem of the Jurisdictional and General Conferences. There are thousands of processes within The United Methodist Church, and all of them are in place to fulfill the mission—making disciples of Jesus Christ. When all the processes are working together toward a common end, the system is in alignment. If all processes are not aligned toward a common end, then the system will not work. In Figure 3A, all processes are linked together.

Systems thinkers state that "the system is designed for the results it is getting." If the system yields the wrong results, it is the wrong system. If all processes do not align toward a common end, the wrong system may be in place.

For more than a generation, mainline denominations have experienced a decline in membership, a decline in average weekly attendance, a decrease in percentage of income giving, and a huge decrease in per capita missions giving. Are these the results we are seeking? Yet these results are what our current system produces. If these are the results we are getting, then our current system is designed to give

Figure 3A

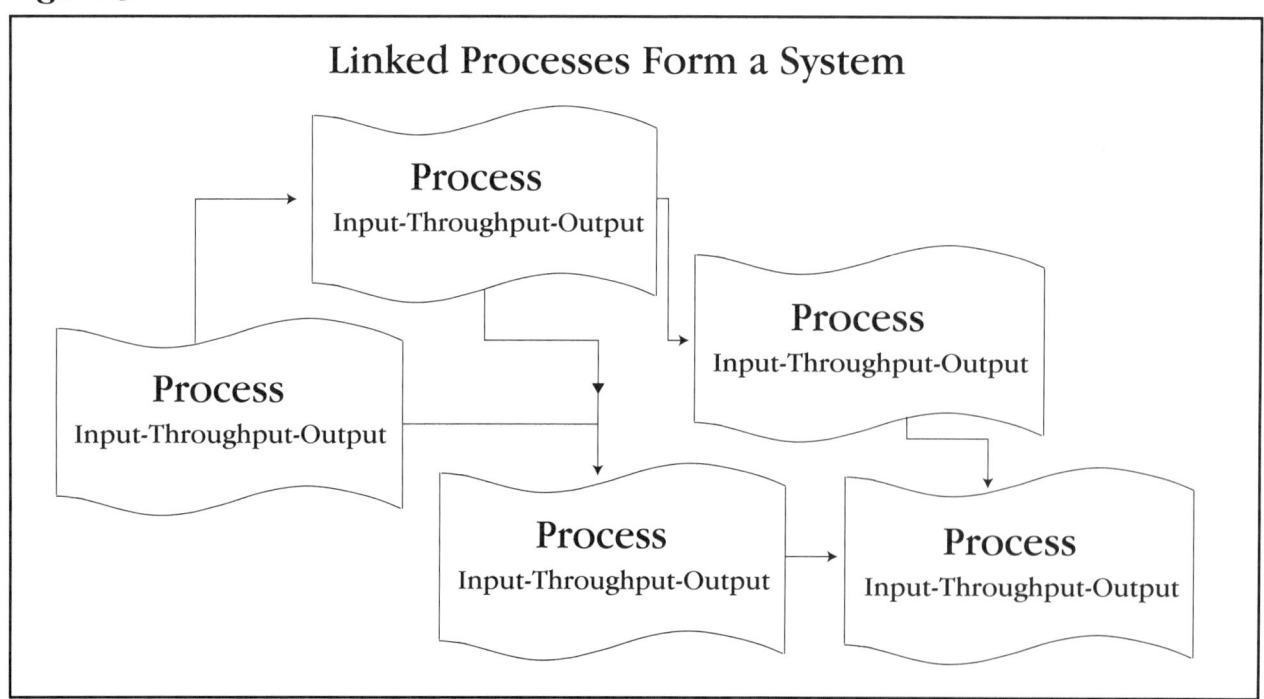

Linked Processes Form a System

Process
Input-Throughput-Output

Process
Input-Throughput-Output

Process
Input-Throughput-Output

Process
Input-Throughput-Output

Process
Input-Throughput-Output

them to us. If it were designed for different results, the system would produce different results. The processes within our congregations are not aligned toward a single goal. Imagine that each arrow in Figure 3C represents a committee working on its own separate goals.

Organizational Structures

Organizational systems don't just happen; they are designed. Processes are developed and organized to achieve certain objectives. Structures are designed to support the system and to align the processes for optimal success. For an organizational structure to be effective, the organization must have clarity about its mission, understand the processes and systems necessary for accomplishing the mission, and align all systems and processes toward the appropriate end. This sounds simpler than it is. If there is confusion about the mission, or if there are conflicting visions for the organization, or if improper processes are joined together to create a bad system, then the organizational structure will not be effective. Often, once an organizational structure is in place, all attention turns to it. If the organization is ineffective, time, effort, and energy are devoted to redesigning the organizational structure. No amount of tinkering with the structure will fix the problem. Only by redesigning the system to align all processes to the mission of the organization will real, productive change occur. An organization is a system of linked processes.

Optimization and Suboptimization

A system is "optimized" when all processes are aligned toward the aim of the organization, as illustrated in Figure 3B. When processes are not aligned, the system is "suboptimized." Leaders within an organization strive to optimize all the processes and systems for the successful fulfillment of the mission. Leaders within local congregations strive to optimize all the processes and systems for ministry to fulfill the mission of the church.

The gospel accounts of the ministry of Jesus Christ reveal the way Jesus moved toward the attainment of his mission. Everything Jesus did supported his mission.

Questions for Discussion

Select one of the following systems:
- Computer
- Orchestra
- School
- Restaurant
- Baseball Team
- Hospital

What are the various processes involved? How do they work together? How would you organize them to optimize the system?

Figure 3B

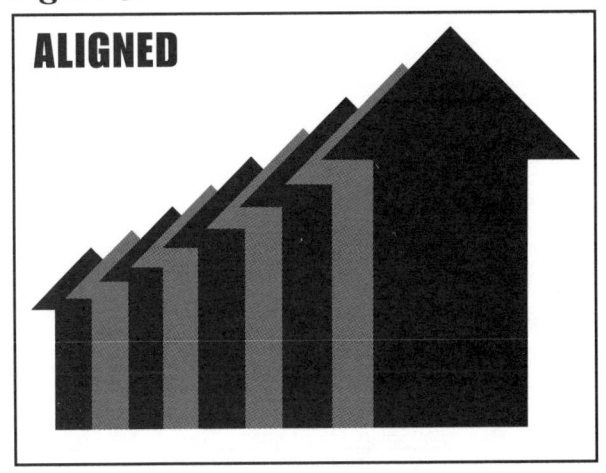

ALIGNED

Figure 3C

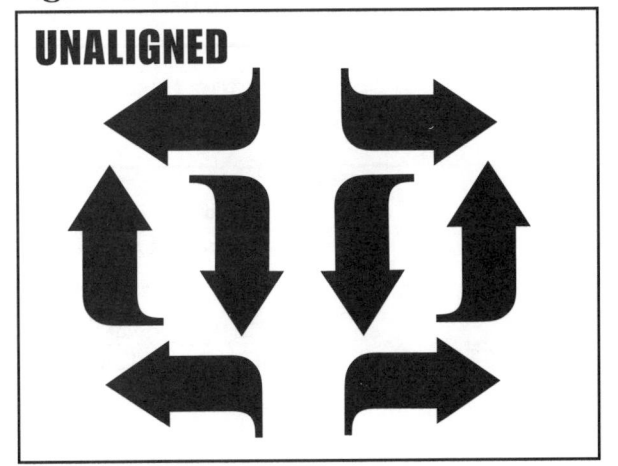

UNALIGNED

Discovery
Naming Our Current Reality

Think about your local church as a system. List all the processes you can think of in the congregation.

Select one of the processes, then fill in the information below.

Is this process aligned with the mission (the desired outcome) of making disciples of Jesus Christ? If any process on your list is not aligned with the mission of the church, why is it important to your church? (Remember, unaligned processes suboptimize the system.)

Here's one example. Think about worship in your church as a subsystem of the larger ministry system. The mission of worship is to make disciples of Jesus Christ. Identify all the different processes in the worship system. What are the inputs, throughputs, and outputs of each process? How are they tied together? Are they all aligned toward the mission of the church?

How do you evaluate which processes optimize the system and which processes suboptimize it?

Systems thinking, being able to see the larger picture rather than focusing on individual parts, is critically important. No individual process occurs apart from any other in an effective system. Worship, evangelism, stewardship, Christian education, missions, and the like are not unrelated programs within the life of the church. Each of these activities contributes to the larger process of disciple making. Each process aligns with every other to attain the common goal, the mission of the church. For too long, clergy and laity have focused attention on one part of the system to the exclusion of others. Worship or education or evangelism becomes "the most important thing." When this happens, the system is suboptimized. Systems thinking moves us beyond viewing the differences among our processes to seeing where they fit together, supporting and sustaining one another.

For Resources, Teaching Aids, and Newest Information

Check out our website at www.faithquest.net.

Figure 3D
PROCESS: _____

INPUTS	THROUGHPUTS	OUTPUTS	OUTCOME
			Making Disciples of Jesus Christ
			Making Disciples of Jesus Christ
			Making Disciples of Jesus Christ
			Making Disciples of Jesus Christ
			Making Disciples of Jesus Christ

SESSION 4:
Leadership in Turbulent Times

Scriptures:
- Luke 5:17-26; 9:1-6; 22:1-38; 23:1-56
  Focus Verses: Luke 22:24-38

Key Biblical Concepts:
- Jesus provides a powerful model for effective leadership
- Jesus delegates and shares authority
- Jesus holds forth the mission and vision for his followers
- Jesus empowers followers to move into leadership roles

Key Concepts for the Journey:
- Characteristics of effective leadership

Outline:
- Gathering
- A Time of Centering
- Prayer
- Preparation
  Questions and Answers
- Exploration
  A Reflective Moment Along the Way
  Questions and Small-Group Exercises
- Discovery
- Conclusion

Introduction

Jesus of Nazareth provides a powerful example of leadership. The lessons to be learned by observing his leadership style are many. In this session, we will look at Jesus, the leader, and explore implications for leadership in the church today.

Prayer

Gracious God, lead us. Teach us how to do the work you have called us to do. Empower us to be effective in our ministry. Remind us that in different ways and in different times, any one of us may emerge as a leader. Help us to use our gifts and abilities in the best possible way, that we might honor and glorify you in all ways. In Jesus' name we pray. Amen.

Preparation
Daily Scripture References and Questions for Reflection

Day 1 — Luke 5:17-26
As an observer of the healing of the paralytic, what do you find remarkable in the behavior of the friends of the man who was paralyzed? Of Jesus?

_____

_____

_____

_____

_____

_____

Day 2 — Luke 9:1-6
What do you think about the instructions that Jesus gives to the disciples in this passage? Why does Jesus give them these instructions? How might they have reacted?

FaithQuest: A New Way of Thinking About Jesus Christ

Day 3 — Luke 22:1-23

How does the story of the Lord's Supper differ from the way we celebrate Communion today? Why is this "Last Supper" so important to Jesus?

Day 4 — Luke 22:24-38

What does Jesus teach the disciples about greatness and leadership?

Day 5 — Luke 23:1-56

How does each of the following define or model leadership for you?

Jesus —

Herod —

Pilate —

Peter —

Judas —

Day 6

Read the session material and make notes in the margins.

Exploration
Background Information: Power and Authority in New Testament Times

The passion story of Jesus Christ has been told many times throughout the centuries. Active church members know the story well and relive its potency each year through Holy Week. The story focuses on the death and resurrection of Jesus so that we might be reconciled to God and inherit eternal life. Indeed, this is the central focus of this story, but there is another dimension that should not be lost.

Jesus of Nazareth, the Christ, completes one phase of his work so that a new phase might begin. The passion story is a story of transition, where the mantle of leadership is passed from the teacher to the disciples. The time of preparation is completed. The journey takes a new turn, and the followers are cast into the role of leaders.

The picture is not a reassuring one. As the leader of the movement moves toward destruction on the cross, the new leaders run, cower, hide, and deny their place in the plan. From an objective point of view, there is strong evidence that the mission of Jesus is going to fail in his absence. But looks can be deceiving.

What constituted effective leadership in Jesus' time is not the same as what constitutes effective leadership today. However, there are some timeless, essential qualities that set Jesus apart. Jesus was a leader ahead of his time.

In Jesus' day, leadership was "top-down" and authoritarian. One person, wielding great power, made decisions and issued orders that were to be carried out without question. Leaders protected themselves by amassing strength and might. The best leader was simply the strongest person. For the most part, leadership was self-serving rather than for the common good. Even within the scriptural accounts of leadership in the Old Testament, might makes right more often than does wisdom or common sense.

Although Jesus held unimaginable power, might did not define his position. Instead, Jesus commanded his authority and power through a single-minded devotion to fulfilling his mission. All his energy and efforts were directed toward designing a lasting system for the completion of his work. Knowing that the work could not be accomplished within one lifetime, Jesus modeled the way through which the kingdom of God could unfold upon the earth. Central to that model was the sharing of leadership with each new generation. The ideas of sharing leadership, empowerment, and planning for the long term were not common leadership traits of the day.

Sadly, they are not much more common in our day; but they are every bit as necessary. The models for leadership provided by Jesus the Christ through the gospel accounts are relevant and timely, and they can guide us toward more effective performance as we lead in the twenty-first century.

A Reflective Moment Along the Way

"A leader is someone you would follow to a place you would not go alone," according to Futurist Joel Barker. Write down the key characteristics of this kind of leader.

During your group session, you may be asked to name characteristics of a good leader. Someone can record the group's list on newsprint. Working together in groups of three or four, think of someone you consider to be an effective leader that "you chose to follow to a place you would not have gone alone." Tell the whole group who you have thought of and why.

Key Concepts for the Journey
Characteristics of Effective Leadership

Leadership is a term that is used in all kinds of settings to mean all kinds of things. Everyone has a vague idea of what leadership is. We can all think of certain leadership qualities we admire. We can all name individuals who, in our opinion, embody effective leadership. Still, there is much debate about leadership.

Are leaders born or made? What is the difference between truly leading and merely filling a leadership role? Is leadership more an art or a science? Is everyone capable of leadership, or is leadership the vocation of the chosen few? Is a leader in one situation necessarily a leader in a different situation? These questions are hotly debated, and no clear answers seem to result. Leadership is an enigma.

We can ill afford to allow leadership to remain enigmatic. Our churches, our schools, our governments, our businesses—indeed, our very world—are crying out for strong, sound, wise leadership. Without good leadership, nothing worthwhile will be accomplished.

This study allows us to examine the model of leadership offered by Jesus the Christ and to reflect on the implications of this model for the work we do as the church.

Jesus embraced five essential qualities of leadership: a strong spiritual center, a clear focus, patience, perseverance, and partnership. He performed four critical tasks: he stated the current reality clearly; he continuously lifted up the vision of the kingdom of God; he modeled the way to move from current reality toward the vision; and he maintained a "big picture," a systems view, of the entire mission.

Strong Spiritual Center

Jesus Christ maintained a strong spiritual center through his relationship with God. Jesus operated out of a prayer base. He was continuously in contact with his spiritual center.

Even nonreligious leaders have a "spiritual" center. Whatever we make sacred in our lives has the power to motivate us. Not all "spiritual centers" are truly worthy, but it is hard to find leaders who do not operate from some core value or center. Without a center, leadership lacks power. In the case of leadership within the church, if our center is not in God, we will not long be effective in our work. As leaders in the church, we are effective only when we are spiritually centered. It is fundamental that leaders ask themselves whether or not they are adequately centered in God. It is important for church leadership teams to examine their spiritual core as well.

Clear Focus

When we examine the gospels, we find that we cannot locate even one instance where Jesus appeared uncertain about his mission. Once his mission was defined, Jesus never wavered from it. Once Jesus "set his face to go to Jerusalem," nothing could sway him. Clarity of focus and commitment to purpose are qualities of good leaders. Jesus never had to ask, "Am I doing the right thing? Is this going to work?" Even in the garden of Gethsemane, when he asked, "Is there another way?" his readiness to finish his course was never in question. Jesus provides a perfect model of focus in leadership.

Patience

Leaders know that long-lasting change takes time. Few things of value happen quickly. Change needs to move through a natural life cycle to be accepted. Personal transformation takes time; hence, effective leaders need to give followers and partners the necessary time to develop and grow. Although a task may be urgent, people must have adequate time to complete the task properly. Jesus was infinitely patient with his disciples and with the mission before him. Although he knew that time was short and that much needed to be accomplished, Jesus created the space necessary for the disciples to mature. True leaders know that there is nothing to be gained by rushing. Quality takes time.

Perseverance

At almost every turn, Jesus encountered some form of opposition: from family, from religious leaders, from government officials, from the wealthy and powerful, and sometimes from the people he served. At times, his own disciples disappointed him; and many times, he seemed all alone in his mission. The pathway to the kingdom of God was a long, arduous one. Occasionally, the journey seemed impossible. In those times, the quality of perseverance appeared.

Perseverance enables us to hold on to what we know to be right and true, even when it is unpopular. Perseverance allows us to go on, even when conventional wisdom tells us to give up. Perseverance makes it possible to accomplish seemingly impossible tasks. Good leaders inspire others to keep on fighting, even beyond the limits of good sense and human endurance.

Partnership

Jesus not only led but also shared leadership with others. No one ever questioned who was in charge, but Jesus often stepped back to allow others to come forward to use their gifts and talents. Jesus was an empowering leader.

Throughout history, leadership has rarely been a solo act. Effective leaders are effective because they are supported by gifted individuals who work together to accomplish a task or goal. Martin Luther King Jr., Mother Theresa, Abraham Lincoln, Alexander the Great, and countless others have attributed their success to the people who worked with them. Leadership is best performed by teams of people, not by individuals. Although Jesus was uniquely suited to lead solo, he chose not to do so. Jesus stood aside while the disciples baptized new followers. Jesus stepped aside to allow his disciples to preach, teach, and heal. Jesus gladly relinquished the spotlight to his partners in ministry. This is a healthy model for our day, when clergy often feel cast in a "lone-ranger" role. Clergy and laity together form the leadership of a local congregation. Any other organizational structure will suboptimize the system. Leaders lead in partnership.

Objective View of Current Reality

An essential task of leadership is to provide an objective view of the way things are. To move forward effectively, an organization has to know its starting place. When we are too close to a situation, we can't see areas that need improvement. Normal becomes good enough, and we lose sight of ways to improve. Leaders never allow good enough to be good enough. Leaders constantly seek ways to become more effective at fulfilling the mission of the organization. Such improvement requires honesty, integrity, and objectivity. Many times, the views of the leaders will not be well received by the members of the organization. Whenever a leader communicates that where we are is not where we ought to be, someone gets defensive. However, good leaders always offer a critical evaluation of current reality to lay a foundation for improvement.

Jesus was an expert at naming current reality. Those who were in positions of power, those who had much to gain by preserving the existent system, were outraged by Jesus' observations. Those who lived outside the circles of power, however, were greatly encouraged by Jesus' honest appraisal of the world. Jesus exposed many customs and practices as ridiculous and wrong.

Vision

Where we are (current reality) is rarely where we really want to be. Vision is where we want to be. It draws us into the future.

Pick up a rubber band. Designate your left thumb as "current reality" and your right thumb as "vision." Now, with the rubber band looped over your thumbs, pull them apart. Feel the tension? A compelling vision provides the tension that pulls us from current reality to a new, better reality. If the vision isn't compelling, there won't be enough tension to move us from where we are. If the vision is too far beyond our reach, the rubber band will snap; and we will be unable to move at all.

Effective leaders listen deeply to the people, gain insight into the visions of their lives, and articulate a shared vision that creates the kind of tension needed to move into the future. Leaders are effective only when they are connected to the deepest desires and yearnings of the people they lead. There is only one way to forge this connection: listening. As leaders listen, they gain perspective about the kind of vision that will touch people's hearts and change their lives.

Leaders who lift up a meaningful and attractive vision will have no problem finding people who will follow. People are looking for meaning and for a way to make a significant contribution in the world. People are ready to follow a powerful vision. Leaders who understand the power of vision will be effective.

A System to Move From Current Reality Toward the Vision

Naming current reality and articulating a vision are ways of identifying starting points and destinations. Leaders are also charged with charting the maps that will move people from their starting point to the desired destination. Leaders must be system designers. This task of devising the means for arriving at an envisioned future truly sets leaders apart from followers. Designing appropriate systems to move from current reality toward a vision requires critical-thinking skills, relationship-building (people) skills, and the ability to align human and material resources toward a common objective. Experience and practice hone these specialized skills. Whether leaders are born with these abilities or learn them along the way, they can always develop and improve.

If the leaders of an organization are unable to develop appropriate systems for moving toward the vision, then the organization will stagnate and, ultimately, fail. For every vision, there is at least one effective way to realize it. It takes creativity, perseverance, teamwork, and patience to find the best way to move from where we are to where we want to be.

Jesus lifted up a number of visions of the kingdom of God that puzzled his followers. As the disciples lived into the visions that Jesus shared, they were able to see the ways that these visions could come to pass. Jesus designed systems that transformed vision from wishful thinking to attainable goals. This is a mark of true leadership.

Stay Focused on the Big Picture

Maintaining a view of the entire system rather than a view of the component parts is not easy. In manufacturing, this overview is known as "walking the catwalk." In a factory, catwalks crisscross the ceiling to enable managers to survey the entire production line below. Walking the catwalk offers the leader a bird's-eye view of the system. Leaders who keep the whole system in view are more concerned with interactions among processes than with the individual processes themselves. When we are focused on individual processes, we may not be able to see where the system breaks down. When we focus on the whole system, it is easier to see where things work well or where they break down.

One district superintendent in The United Methodist Church reflects on a key learning she received early in her appointment. As she traveled her circuit of charge conferences, she measured membership and worship attendance over a three-year period to see whether or not a church was growing. At one small rural church, she was alarmed to see an eighty percent drop in Sunday morning worship attendance, from 120 per week to just 24 per week—in less than two years. As she began to lecture the members of the charge conference, a laywoman from the congregation interrupted her. The woman said that in the past two years, this small church had created a number of small groups for study, fellowship, and worship. She pointed out that the congregation was active seven days a week, instead of just one. More than 200 people were involved in the church each week, and the income to the budget had increased by more than 75 percent in one year. This same woman reported that the church was stronger than at any time in its history, although few people attended on Sunday morning. The district superintendent received a graphic illustration of what happens when a person fails to take a systems approach to the church. Individual processes tell incomplete stories. Only when viewed within the larger context can individual processes yield usable information.

We have outlined some of the key qualities and tasks of effective leaders. Leadership is critical to the health and well-being of any organization. Leadership is everyone's responsibility. Even though not every person is gifted in leadership, every person has the obligation to demand quality leadership and to strive to make training and resources available to strengthen the leaders who are present. We cannot lament the condition of leadership in our church unless we are willing to make the sacrifices necessary to develop quality leaders for the future. The decision is ours.

Moving to the faith-forming-community paradigm will require effective leadership. We will be moving into uncharted territory, where difficult decisions will have to be made. It takes courage to name the current reality, especially when it challenges long-held beliefs and practices. There is great risk in holding forth a new vision and in designing different systems for ministry. It is uncomfortable to leave what is known for what is unknown. Yet, this is what leadership is all about. If we didn't need to move, there would be no need for anyone to lead.

Questions for Discussion

What is the difference between effective leadership and being an effective leader?

What qualities and characteristics of effective leadership were not mentioned in this session?

What critical leadership qualities are needed to create faith-forming communities?

Discuss ways in which leadership is an art; a science; an inherent ability.

Discovery
Naming Our Current Reality

By their ordination and appointment, pastors are the designated leaders in local congregations. However, the leadership *role* says nothing about leadership *ability*. Many lay leaders are resident in every local congregation. The most effective congregations will be those that craft a dynamic leadership team that uses the gifts and abilities of both clergy and laity. The mission of the church is too large for one person to assume total responsibility. There is no place for "lone-ranger" leaders in the church of the twenty-first century.

What is the process in your church for discovering, developing, and using the leaders of your congregation? How do you identify gifts for ministry and service?

What leadership qualities does your congregation most value in its clergy leaders? In its laity leaders? (If they are different, why are they different?)

How have the qualities of effective leadership evolved in the last generation? What styles of leadership are no longer appropriate?

Session 4: Leadership in Turbulent Times

_____
_____
_____
_____
_____

Exercise

Figure 4A shows four distinct leadership roles. Every person fits into all four categories to some degree, and we may move from one role to another depending on the situation.

Advisors are observers of the process who stay focused on the big picture. They help an organization get the most out of its human and material resources. Advisors don't make decisions; they offer suggestions. They don't solve problems; they offer alternatives. They might share in doing the work, but they usually spend more time seeking ways to improve the processes for performing work.

Owners are those people who take responsibility for the success or failure of a project. In a committee or team, every person needs to take ownership of all work to guarantee success. Ownership needs to be spread over the widest number of people.

Implementers make the work happen. They make decisions, delegate responsibility, and perform specific tasks. Implementers tend to have specialized skills.

Innovators and *designers* are idea people. They generate new concepts, solve problems, and improve processes. These creative minds are few and far between, and it is important to free them from detail work so that they may optimize their contribution to the organization.

Which role is the most appropriate for the clergy leaders in your congregation? Why? (Please choose only one.)

What happens when a single leader is responsible for more than one leadership function or role? What are the possible dangers?

What will these roles look like in a congregation that is moving into the faith-forming-community paradigm?

What are the implications of these roles for the committee on lay leadership in your congregation?

For Resources, Teaching Aids, and Newest Information

Check out our website at www.faithquest.net.

Figure 4A

LEADERSHIP ROLES

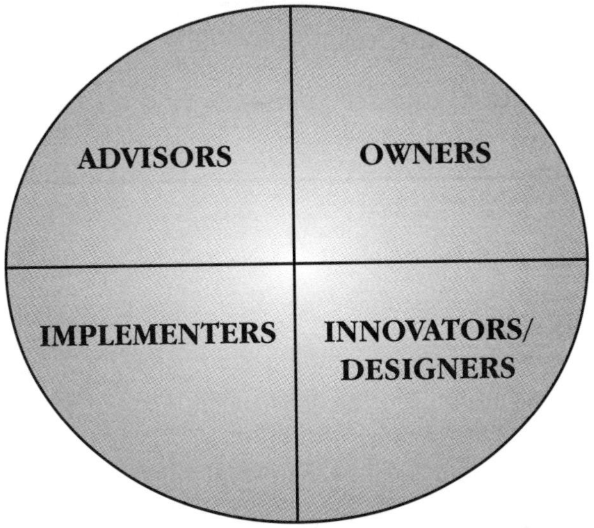

[Circle divided into four quadrants: ADVISORS, OWNERS, IMPLEMENTERS, INNOVATORS/DESIGNERS]

Advisors–offer perspective and advice on a process or project.

Owners–take responsibility for the success or failure of a process or project.

Implementers–make a process or project happen. Implementers do the work.

Innovators/Designers–create new ideas and design processes and projects.

SESSION 5:
The Power of the Resurrection

Scriptures:
- Luke 7:24-35; 8:4-15; 24:1-53; 1:46-55
  Focus Verses: Luke 8:4-8

Key Biblical Concepts:
- God has a plan for the church
- God's people need to tend to the mission of the church and let God worry about the results
- We are witnesses to the truth of Jesus Christ
- We have a wonderful message to share

Key Concepts for the Journey:
- Primary task
- Flow
- Constraints

Outline:
- Gathering
- A Time of Centering
- Prayer
- Preparation
  Questions and Answers
- Exploration
  A Reflective Moment Along the Way
  Questions and Small-Group Exercises
- Discovery
- Conclusion

Introduction

The resurrection of Jesus Christ was the turning point of history. In this event, the paradigm shifted once and for all. A new relationship developed between God and humankind. The kingdom of God became the vision for a new church. All who would follow the apostles of Jesus Christ would experience a new reality, and they would participate in the grand work of preaching the good news of repentance and forgiveness to a lost and lonely world.

This session will revisit the Resurrection event and will explore what it means to be disciples at the start of the twenty-first century.

Prayer

Almighty God, we rejoice that we are your people, saved and redeemed by the resurrection of your Son, Jesus Christ. Motivate us to share the dual message of redemption and salvation in our world today. Give us a vision for the best way that we can communicate your good news. Sharpen our focus upon the main message, that we might ever be ready to share it, wherever we might be. We ask this in Jesus' name. Amen.

Preparation
Daily Scripture References and Questions for Reflection

Day 1 — Luke 7:24-35
What did people seek from John the Baptist when they found him in the wilderness? How did the lawyers and Pharisees reject God's purpose for their lives by refusing the baptism of John?

_____

_____

_____

_____

_____

Day 2 — Luke 8:4-8
What is the primary work of the sower in the parable? How does a sower measure success?

_____
_____
_____
_____
_____

Day 3 — Luke 24:1-12
What is the message of the women who first visited the tomb of Jesus? How did the apostles respond to the story the women told?

_____
_____
_____
_____
_____

Day 4 — Luke 24:13-53
What was the effect of Jesus' appearance on the road to Emmaus (Luke 24:13-35)? What was the impact of the Resurrection upon the disciples (Luke 24:36-51)? What did the disciples do in response to Jesus' post-Resurrection appearances?

_____
_____
_____
_____

Day 5 — Luke 1:46-55
How is Mary's song of praise our song of praise today? What is the relationship between Mary's song and the meaning of Resurrection?

_____
_____
_____
_____
_____
_____

Day 6
Read the session material and make notes in the margins.

Exploration
Background Information: The Event That Makes Jesus Different

Many came claiming to be sons and daughters of God. Many came healing, performing miracles, and proclaiming all forms of good news. Many came challenging the established order of the day. Many came making claims to messianic glory, but only one died and then returned. The Resurrection is the key event that set Jesus apart and that set in motion the establishment of an entirely new religion. Witnesses to the risen Christ traveled far and wide with the message "We have seen the Lord!" The Resurrection was confirmation of the good news of God's redemption and salvation.

It is ironic that the modern-day church takes the resurrection of Jesus Christ for granted, almost as if resurrection is the most ordinary thing in the world. The power, the mystery, the magic has somehow been lost because we have grown up with the truth of the event. Think about the shock that it caused the followers of Jesus. Even his closest friends, the disciples, had difficulty accepting the truth of the Resurrection. Jesus repeatedly taught the disciples that he must die and return from the dead to fulfill God's plan. Even with such instruction, the Twelve were not prepared for what happened.

When the women returned from the tomb, skepticism was the order of the day; Peter had to check it out for himself. Even with these experiences, the disciples still kept themselves locked away until the emissaries from the Emmaus road experience brought further confirmation. Resurrection is anything but ordinary. Even the most faithful have difficulties accepting the return of one known dead.

Once the disciples experienced the risen Christ, they were forever transformed. Gone were the last vestiges of doubt. Gone were the concerns for personal safety and well-being. Gone were the aspirations to greatness and glory. Instead, the risen Christ provided the disciples with the confidence and courage to take up the mantle of leadership—to be the church for the world.

The Christian church is the church of the Resurrection. It is by this incredible act that we have the gospel to share. It is only as we experience the power and majesty of this miracle that we, too, receive the confidence and conviction to carry the good news to the world. Jesus Christ died for our sins. Jesus Christ rose again, transforming our sin into God's salvation.

Salvation History

The Gospel of Luke is not history in the classic sense. Its intention is not to recount the exact occurrences of the day. Instead, Luke tells a story and uses historic, factual events to support it. The author is an evangelist, and he begins first with the message he wants to communicate. The Gospel of Luke is not a writing of history, but a writing of *salvation* history. Luke tells the story of Jesus Christ, who came to save all humankind and to institute the kingdom of God in the world. Jesus came to offer salvation to all who would listen—even to those to whom salvation had been denied in the past, the Gentiles. As we move from the Gospel of Luke to the Book of Acts, we will see how the good news of salvation moved beyond Jerusalem to the ends of the known world. The Gospel of Luke is a story of redemption and salvation.

The gospel also recounts a cultural paradigm shift. Luke's story is one of justice and hope for the poor, the weak, the sick, the outcast, and the dispossessed. Never before had the story of God's justice been so readily shared with the marginalized of society. It is ironic that the leadership of the Hebrew people, so well versed in the pain and suffering of being oppressed, should so readily oppress so many in their homeland. Jesus took delight in pointing out this contradiction. Jesus was a champion of the underdog, and Luke's Gospel is the record of that relationship.

Ultimately, the Gospel of Luke offers a simple message: rejoice, for the lost are lost no more. Salvation comes to all, beginning with the least of all, extending to anyone who will receive it. This is good news!

A Reflective Moment Along the Way

The resurrection of Jesus was the physical evidence that God's plan for the salvation of the world could not be thwarted. The proclamation of God's victory over sin and death became the focus of the early church. The key concept of this session is the importance of the church's "primary task." In Session 2 you read that the mission of The United Methodist Church as described in our *Book of Discipline* is to make disciples of Jesus Christ. Reread Luke 24:44-49 and Matthew 28:18-20. Both of these commands are given by a victorious, resurrected Jesus, who now must depend upon his disciples to proclaim the message of the mission. That includes us!

Reflect on these questions as you prepare for your group meeting. You can write notes in the margin. Is the idea of our primary task of "making disciples for Jesus Christ in order to transform the world" a new idea for you? For your church? How would you imagine most of your congregation would respond if you asked them to state the mission of the church?

Key Concepts for the Journey
Primary Task

Phil opened a coffee shop. In a short time, Phil's Place was a popular hangout, and it did a booming business. Someone suggested to Phil that he should also sell tea and pastries and bagels. Phil, always wanting to please the customers, expanded his offerings. Others thought that Phil should carry a variety of newspapers so that they could pick up the paper when they got coffee. Some folks who spent a lot of time at Phil's thought he should offer live music a couple of evenings each week. More and more suggestions came in, and Phil attempted to respond to them all. Ironically, as Phil offered more goods and services, customer traffic decreased. The reason? As the shop offered more and different products and services, the quality of the coffee declined. At times, Phil's ran out of coffee because no one had time to make a fresh urn. People had to wait for fresh coffee. People who were looking to grab a quick cup on their way to work got caught behind lines of people ordering pastries and papers. Phil, in his desire to please everyone, forgot something essential: His business was popular because it sold coffee. It was a coffee shop. Phil forgot to stay focused on his primary task.

The primary task is the one thing we must do to stay in business. It is important to define a mission, and it is critical to have a vision; but unless you stay focused on the system for getting from current reality to that vision, you will not survive. In business, this is called the core process—the fundamental process upon which all other processes depend. Every system has a core process or primary task. Without a primary task, the system will fail.

We have defined the mission of The United Methodist Church as "making disciples of Jesus Christ." Each local church is a system designed to achieve that mission. Each congregation develops a unique and compelling vision for realizing that mission. Is there a core process or primary task that each church must contain to be effective? Our *Book of Discipline* states that the core "Process for Carrying Out Our Mission" is to:

—proclaim the gospel, seek, welcome and gather persons into the body of Christ;
—lead persons to commit their lives to God through baptism and profession of faith in Jesus Christ;
—nurture persons in Christian living through worship, the sacraments, spiritual disciplines, and other means of grace, such as Wesley's Christian conferencing;
—send persons into the world to live lovingly and justly as servants of Christ by healing the sick, feeding the hungry, caring for the stranger, freeing the oppressed, and working to develop social structures that are consistent with the gospel; and
—[gather feedback and] continue the mission of seeking, welcoming and gathering persons into the community of the body of Christ.[3]

Each aspect of the primary task (see Figure 5A) needs to be fully functioning to optimize the system. The success of the primary task depends on unrestricted flow through each step of the process. Any constraint in any of the processes will suboptimize the entire disciple-making system.

Flow

Flow is a concept that is rarely considered—until it breaks down. Think about a river. The water moves from a source to a destination. This is called "destination flow," and there is a distinct starting and ending point. The process is completed when the destination is reached.

Destination flow may also be "directional flow," but directional flow is not necessarily destination flow. Destination flow always has an end point, and it moves in one direction to that point. Destination flow is defined by its end point; directional flow, by its movement.

Traffic on a one-way street is an example of directional flow. Manufacturing depends on directional flow. Each product moves along an assembly line to completion.

Another type of flow is "pendulum flow." Examples of pendulum flow are weekly trips to the supermarket, the bank, the post office, or even to church. We begin from our home source, travel to a destination, and return. The process is a swing back and forth—like a pendulum. The system is designed to repeat the same process over and over.

These three types of flow work on closed systems. They are linear and move toward specific objectives. A fourth type of flow is at work in an open system—"spiral flow."

Disciple-making calls for spiral flow, where there is no definite end point. The system exists to perpetuate an ongoing process. The primary task of The United Methodist Church requires spiral flow. If our mission is anything less than making disciples of Jesus Christ, we may find ourselves experiencing

Session 5: The Power of the Resurrection

PRIMARY TASK OF THE UNITED METHODIST CHURCH

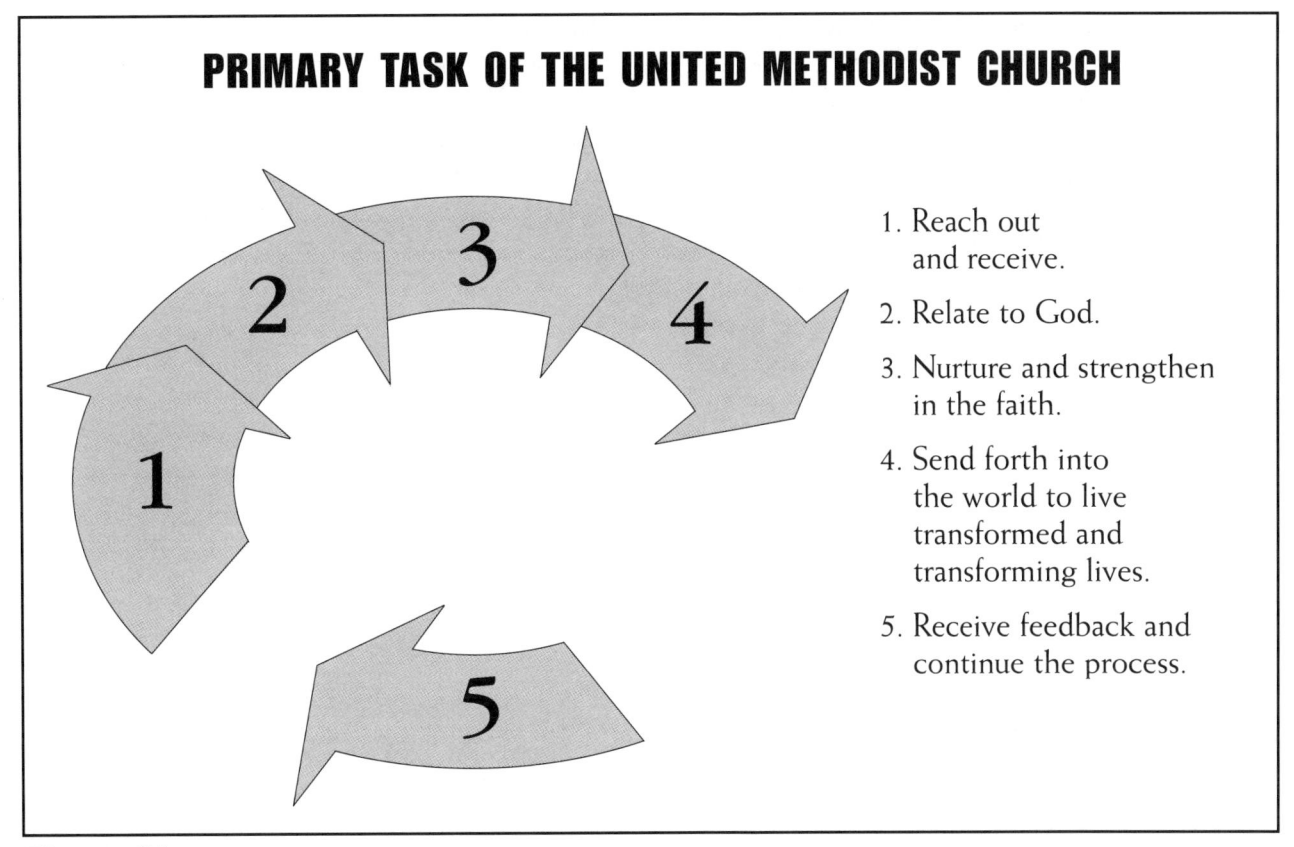

1. Reach out and receive.
2. Relate to God.
3. Nurture and strengthen in the faith.
4. Send forth into the world to live transformed and transforming lives.
5. Receive feedback and continue the process.

Figure 5A

the wrong kind of flow. Making church members requires destination flow (getting people to the destination of the church). Confirming youngsters depends on directional flow (as they are moved through the system). Keeping attendance up (and encouraging people to return week after week) requires pendulum flow. If the congregation becomes inwardly focused, any of these types of flow might suffice. But the primary task—what the church must do to be the church—will be compromised. To fulfill the mission of the church by attending to the primary task, we must create a spiral flow.

Spiral flow continuously moves forward and upward. We never reach a destination because there is always a next level. Once we have received seekers into the fellowship, have related them to God, have effectively nurtured and strengthened them in their faith, and have sent them forth to live as Christian disciples in the world, both we and they have the opportunity to begin the process all over again. Each time we participate in the primary task of the church, we grow in our discipleship. We move along a spiral of growth and development in our faithfulness, and we strengthen the disciple-making system of our church. When everyone is aligned with the primary task of the congregation, the system functions well. Everyone needs to look for possible constraints in the system.

Constraints

A man was having a difficult time washing his car. Every time he turned the hose on the automobile, his daughter crept up behind him, grabbed the hose, and put a kink in it. As the hose was folded over, the water was blocked. The man's daughter created a *constraint* in the water-flow system.

Anything that impedes flow is a constraint. A constraint in just one process can undermine the entire system. Often, we look for many different reasons why a system is ineffective. Many times, the poor performance of a system can be traced back to a single constraint. When an organization fails in its mission, very often there is a constraint in the core process. This breaks the flow, and effectiveness is impossible.

The primary task of The United Methodist Church involves five processes that create a spiral flow. The ability to relate people to God depends on effectively reaching out and receiving people into the community of faith. Until people are introduced to the Christian faith, they cannot be nurtured or strengthened in it. Without growth and development in the faith, individuals will not be empowered to live Christian lives in the world. It is in the power of faithful Christian discipleship that people are motivated to reach out and to invite others to join the community of faith. It is easy to see how a constraint in any one of these processes could destroy the disciple-making system of the church.

Questions for Discussion

How does the salvation history of the Gospel of Luke find expression in the primary task of The United Methodist Church? How does the primary task help define the work of Christian disciples?

What does it mean to be a "witness of the Resurrection" in the twenty-first century? How can we rekindle the power and motivation of the resurrection of Jesus the Christ in our day?

_____

_____

_____

_____

_____

Discovery
Naming Our Current Reality

The primary task of The United Methodist Church is the core process of the disciple-making system. Each step of the core process is interrelated. We must be careful not to focus on one step to the exclusion of any other. Systems thinking and the leadership role of "walking the catwalk" will prevent this from happening.

It would be easy to look at the steps of the primary task and say, "Well, reaching out and receiving is the work of the evangelism committee, and relating people to God is the work of the worship committee, and Christian education nurtures and strengthens people in the faith, and the missions committee and church and society committee allow people to put their faith into action." These comments miss the point. We do not attach committees to the steps of the primary task. The primary task is the core process of *everything* we do in the church. It is more appropriate to ask, "How does our worship ministry group make sure that the flow of the primary task is constraint-free? How do we reach out and receive people, relate them to God, nurture and strengthen them in their faith, send them forth to live as disciples, and enable them to reach out and receive others through our worship experiences?"

Exercise

Figure 5B looks at the church in the activity-center paradigm model. Each of the processes of our primary task heads a column. The rows represent committees a congregation might have to carry out the task of ministry. Reproduce Figure 5B on newsprint, listing your standing committees in the first column. Fill in the spaces to describe how each committee serves the primary task in this model.

Now do the same for Figure 5C, which shows the church as a "faith-forming community" paradigm model. On this chart, rather than focusing on committees, the means of grace become the processes to fulfill the primary task.

Compare the two charts. What differences do you see? How does the focus of the church change in each model? What are the implications of each "system"?

For Resources, Teaching Aids, and Newest Information

Check out our website at www.faithquest.net.

Session 5: The Power of the Resurrection

ACTIVITY CENTER					
	Reach Out and Receive	Relate to God in Jesus Christ	Nurture and Strengthen in the Faith	Send Forth to Live as Christian Disciples	Continue the Work of Invitation in the World
Worship					
Evangelism					
Stewardship					
Education					
Missions					
Trustees					
Youth					
Women					
Men					
Finance					

Figure 5B

FAITH-FORMING CENTER					
	Reach Out and Receive	Relate to God in Jesus Christ	Nurture and Strengthen in the Faith	Send Forth to Live as Christian Disciples	Continue the Work of Invitation in the World
Prayer					
Study of Scripture					
Lord's Supper					
Fasting					
Christian Conference					
Acts of Mercy					

Figure 5C

when a customer receives better service, better products, better attention, and better quality from one particular provider, then that customer will return to that provider. The third level of quality creates a solid foundation for building lasting relationships.

Questions for Discussion

What are the implications of a focus on customers and quality in the church? How does our understanding of the church change if we view one another as customers?

In what ways does the church provide services that reflect the three levels of quality? How can we move from first- and second-level quality (assumed and desired) to the third level of quality (unexpected)?

_____

_____

_____

_____

Discovery
Naming Our Current Reality: Who Are Our Customers?

Customers are the people we serve. Management science identifies five categories of customers:

(1) workers, (2) owners, (3) beneficiaries, (4) suppliers, and (5) the community.

Workers are those who make things, create ideas, and provide services. Owners are those who own businesses or factories. Beneficiaries are the people who benefit from products, goods, and services. Suppliers provide the raw materials and machinery. The community benefits from jobs and services provided. Let's explore how this might apply to the people we serve in the faith community.

Exercise

Reread Acts 6:1-7. Discuss the importance of listening to the customers in this example. Remember and name some Gospel stories in which Jesus "listened" to the people he served (customers). Discuss Jesus' response to each situation in these stories.

Next, reflect on: Who were the workers that Jesus served? The owners? Beneficiaries? Suppliers? Community? (Name as many as you can in each category.)

Think of the customers of your local church. Who are the workers you serve? The owners? Beneficiaries? Suppliers? Community? (Name as many as you can in each category.)

How do you listen to the customers in each category? When leaders fail to listen to *all* the customers, they suboptimize the system for ministry. What steps does your church need to take to listen to all its customers?

For Resources, Teaching Aids, and Newest Information

Check out our website at www.faithquest.net.

SESSION 8:
The Road to Transformation

Scriptures:
- Acts 8:1–12:25
  Focus Verses: Acts 9:1-19a

Key Biblical Concepts:
- Christ has the power to change lives
- Baptism
- Everyone is acceptable in the kingdom of God
- Antioch is the birthplace of Christianity

Key Concepts for the Journey:
- Paradigm thinking
- Change readiness

Outline:
- Gathering
- A Time of Centering
- Prayer
- Preparation
  Questions and Answers
- Exploration
  A Reflective Moment Along the Way
  Questions and Small-Group Exercises
- Discovery
- Conclusion

Prayer

Too often we are blinded by our own short-sighted opinions and prejudices, O Lord. We need to see through new eyes. Enable us to take nothing for granted. Help us to seek better ways to live in the world and to relate to other people. Help us to exemplify the kingdom of God through all that we say and all that we do, that we might honor and glorify you in the name of Jesus Christ. Amen.

Preparation
Daily Scripture References and Questions for Reflection

Day 1 — Acts 8:4-40
How do the apostles deal with the magician and the eunuch? What is the difference between baptism in the name of Jesus and baptism in the Holy Spirit?

_____

_____

_____

_____

_____

Day 2 — Acts 8:1b-3, 9:1-19a
What stands out in the story of Saul's conversion? What is God's intention for Saul?

_____

_____

Introduction

A new day dawns for the people of God as converted Jews and Gentiles form a whole new kind of community. Christ is the unifying factor that allows hated enemies to become brothers and sisters. Although there is incredible resistance to the new church, the momentum builds as the Kingdom is revealed.

Day 3 — Acts 9:19b-31

How did Saul come to be accepted by the apostles? Why did both the Jewish and Hellenistic leaders seek to kill him?

Day 4 — Acts 9:32–11:18

What changes did Peter have to make to take the gospel into the Gentile world? How is Peter received when he returns to Jerusalem?

Day 5 — Acts 11:19–12:25

What is unique about the Christian community described in Antioch? Why does the growth of the Antioch community result in increased persecution of Christian leaders?

Day 6

Read the session material and make notes in the margin.

Exploration
Background Information: The Gentile World

The Book of Acts is a grand epic of reconciliation and redemption. In the panorama of Luke through Acts, the gospel takes root in Jerusalem, spreads throughout Judea, on to Samaria, and finally to the entire Gentile world. The relationship between the Jews and Samaritans is legendary. From the tale of the good Samaritan, we are reminded of the utter hatred the descendants of the Northern Kingdoms elicited from the Southern Jews. This animosity grew through the centuries, but it held no comparison to the utter contempt and distaste that the Jews held for the Gentiles.

The Jews viewed the Gentiles as unclean, barbaric, unholy, ignorant, sinful, and eternally condemned. The chosen people lived with total assurance that they were the rightful heirs of creation and that the Gentiles had no significance. The fact that the Gentiles had oppressed the people of God throughout history only confirmed the Gentiles' fallen state. Jews could keep themselves pure only to the extent that they refrained from interacting with Gentiles. Mere contact with Gentiles meant defilement and the need to be purged and cleansed. In the created order, no one held a lower position in the minds and hearts of the Hebrew people than the Gentiles.

We can hardly fathom what an incredible change of heart was required for Jewish converts to be willing to share their faith with the Gentile world. It is proof of the transforming might of the Holy Spirit that this change happened virtually instantaneously. There were some difficult moments and temporary lapses, as evidenced by Peter, but the former Jews did an amazing job of breaking with past resentments and anger to open the Christian good news to the rest of the world. When they called for repentance and proclaimed the forgiveness of God, they encountered an open and accepting audience.

It is notable that Christ was still working with the stiff-necked Peter to bend him to worldwide service. Peter held old views about clean and unclean, sacred and profane. The story of Peter in the home of Simon the tanner and the subsequent vision is critically important. This is a clear message that those who carry the gospel to other people must meet those people where they are. Judging and setting hard and fast rules are at odds with the core of the gospel. The good news is about forgiveness and reconciliation. Laws and rules separate people. Grace brings people together and enables them to look past their differences. In the Book of Acts, the community of Christian belief extends to magicians and eunuchs. Anyone who is willing to claim Jesus Christ as Lord and Savior is acceptable in the eyes of God. Peter held notions of imposing Jewish standards of conduct and acceptability on the Gentile world. Jesus Christ had other ideas. In a wondrous and powerful way, Christ sent the communication to Peter that what God finds acceptable, no mortal may judge as unacceptable. This directive could be applied widely in our own day.

Antioch stands out as a crossroads in history. The church may have been born at Pentecost, but Christianity as a distinct movement was born in Antioch. The support for such a claim? Antioch is the first location of a blended community of Jewish and Gentile converts, together as a new entity. Here, two traditions, two backgrounds, two belief systems merged. The integrity of this community frightened the leaders of the day. They felt it necessary to stem the tide of movement toward Christian community. Persecution of the apostles and converts to the faith intensified shortly after the successful establishment of the Christian church in Antioch.

Baptism

The Book of Acts raises some debates about baptism. The baptism of John the Baptist and the twelve disciples was a washing away of sins and an act of repentance and contrition. Jesus proclaimed another baptism, one of the Spirit. The Book of Acts refers to both baptisms: a baptism in the name of Jesus Christ and a baptism in the Holy Spirit. Baptism, at different times in Acts, is presented as a washing away of sins, a confirmation of God's saving grace, an initiation into a new community, an empowerment for service, and a spiritual transformation. On at least one occasion, the baptism of the Holy Spirit precedes water baptism. In other situations, there is no mention of the baptism of the Spirit following water baptism.

In our day, there is danger of reducing baptism to little more than an act of Christian initiation. This misses the point—and the spirit—of the symbolic nature of baptism to the primitive church. Water baptism was to baptism by the Holy Spirit what conception is to birth. Water baptism did not merely introduce a new convert into community in Christ, it also planted seeds of the Spirit that set the individual apart for God. It is significant that baptism was quickly extended to women in the early Christian movement. Baptism was empowerment. Baptism was a promotion to the ranks of servants sharing in the proclamation of the good news. The baptized were connected to the mystical body of Christ and were gifted for service. More than initiation, baptism was an experience of radical transformation. Baptism defined the newly emerging church in a powerful way. Water baptism was a response to the saving gift of God; Spirit baptism was confirmation of that salvation.

A Reflective Moment Along the Way

Becoming a faith community requires that people grow in the knowledge of one another. As the community grows, so do the faith stories of that community. The Bible is full of such faith stories that have become foundational pillars for the people of God through the centuries. Perhaps by the end of this Bible study, your group will begin to treasure faith stories of your encounters with the living presence of God.

Remember your own favorite Bible story or passage. Why is it your favorite? When you meet together, listen to the choices each person names. After everyone has spoken, try to identify one new insight you have gained into the hearts of the other people in your small group. In what other church setting might such an exercise help your church develop faith-forming community?

Key Concepts for the Journey
Paradigm Thinking

As defined in Session 1, paradigms are sets of assumptions, rules, opinions, and ideas that describe reality. Christianity is a paradigm: a set of beliefs, assumptions, practices, rules, and opinions that people choose or refuse to live within. Contained within Christianity are other paradigms.

C. Jeff Woods, in his book *Congregational Megatrends*, identifies a number of paradigm shifts that affect the church.[5] A generation ago, people primarily expressed their faith through connection with a church. Today, people are aligning themselves more with a way of thinking or believing than with an institution. As established churches struggle to attract new members, interest in angels, spiritual gifts, crystals, heaven, mind power, reincarnation, eastern beliefs, and magic increases daily. People describe themselves as spiritual rather than religious. Paradigms are shifting. It is important to be aware of paradigms as they shift to know how to respond to them.

When such external change occurs, we have little control over it. The best we can do in the face of these significant shifts is to identify them and be ready to respond.

There are, however, some paradigms over which we do have control. These are assumptions, rules, opinions, or ideas that fall within the limits of our command. The ways we look at the world, the rules under which we operate, are personal paradigms. We hold these individually and corporately.

Think about the paradigm of improving the quality of experience people have in our congregations. If we decide to provide quality to the people we serve, then that commitment will influence everything we do. We will look for new and innovative ways to improve worship, education, fellowship, and faith formation. We will strive to delight people (the third level of quality as described in Session 7) to make sure that they need look no further than our faith community. Operating from a quality paradigm, we will be more sensitive to areas of poor quality. We will begin to see evidence of the three levels of quality everywhere we look. We will begin to demand high quality because we know such quality is possible. In time, we will never offer poor quality again. We adopt this paradigm and commit to it.

Consider the paradigm of including all people in our congregations. The books of Luke and Acts define the mission of Christ and the church as a universal mission: salvation for all. These two writings present a global paradigm in which everyone is acceptable. If we were to adopt this inclusiveness paradigm, we would design systems for ministry that make no distinctions. We would be open to rich or poor, well or ill, old or young, men, women, and children. No one would be considered of lesser value than anyone else. We would have racial, ethnic, generational, and gender inclusiveness. No one would feel left out because no one would be left out. We would seek new audiences (customer groups) to serve. We would be vigilant for ways to connect more people to our community of faith. Once more, this is a paradigm over which we have control.

So, how do we prepare to respond to changes of both kinds, those that we have little or no control over and those that we do have control over? We need a new way of thinking, which we will call "paradigm thinking." It's a way of thinking that enables us to embrace change rather than resist it.

Change Readiness

Paradigm thinking is a model (set of rules and assumptions) for becoming "change ready." Here are five rules that can help an individual or group respond to and embrace change: (1) challenge all assumptions; (2) explore alternatives; (3) adopt other points of view; (4) read extensively outside your area of expertise; and (5) find success in every attempt.

Challenge All Assumptions

To assume something means to take it for granted. I may assume that my wife will lock the door at night. I may assume that she will pick up my son from school. I may assume that she will go to the grocery store. I assume these things based on past experience, patterns, practices, and a wide variety of spoken and unspoken agreements.

If I married a different person, should I make the same assumptions about my new wife? Of course not. I shouldn't even make assumptions with the wife I have!

Assumptions are suppositions that may or may not have a basis in fact. Assumptions are unverified and are nonverifiable until after the fact.

We sometimes assume that we know why people come to church, what they like in worship, what missions they will support, or what programs they will attend. These assumptions may be rooted in past experience, observation of what other churches do, or personal opinion; or they may be based on a small sample of the larger congregation. The only way to verify assumptions is to air them publicly and to ask people to respond to them. No assumption should go unchallenged. Challenging assumptions is an excellent way to listen to the people we serve.

Explore Alternatives

"There is one best way to run a church supper."

"We use a standard design for the worship bulletin."

"Everyone wants a copy of the church budget."

These are some assumptions that need testing. One good way to test assumptions is to explore alternatives.

One church served its suppers family-style for forty years. The church offered three seatings and served about 180 people. When the young adults held the supper and served it cafeteria-style, they served 340 people and made over $2000 more than other church suppers.

Another church had its worship bulletins printed the same way for years. One day, a church member noticed that newcomers and visitors didn't participate at all points in the service. She talked with some of them and learned that they were confused and couldn't follow the order of worship printed in the bulletin.

A church that dutifully passed out copies of its annual budget decided one year just to print a stack and make them available to anyone who desired a copy. Imagine the surprise when only five copies were taken!

For every act we perform in our churches, we have a variety of alternatives. We sometimes get into the habit of doing the same thing the same way over and over again. It is foolish to keep doing the same thing again and again and to expect different results. There is no guarantee that because something was effective in one time or place that it will be effective again. In an age of constantly shifting paradigms, we can't afford not to explore options.

Adopt Other Points of View

Paradigm thinking requires the ability to see from various perspectives. In every situation, the people involved often have distinctly different points of view. It is helpful to step back from a discussion or project and to try to put yourself in another person's position. Instead of attempting to sway other people to your point of view, seek first to understand theirs.

One pastor who wanted her church to adopt a contemporary worship service could not understand why there was such resistance. She kept singing the praises of new music and new liturgy and drama and interpretive dance, but the more she talked, the more she met barriers. She asked herself, "How would I feel if I were in their shoes?" She began to see that some people were afraid of change. Some feared that they might lose the traditional worship that meant so much to them. Some were concerned that a flood of newcomers would make the church too big. Some people felt that the new methods of worship were inappropriate. By adopting a variety of points of view, this pastor was able to address specific issues of resistance and to reassure her congregation that all would be well. By seeing the issue from several perspectives, the pastor was able to help the congregation accept change.

It costs little to see things from other people's points of view, but the benefits can be priceless.

Read Extensively Outside Your Area of Expertise

Jesus didn't use religious images to communicate deep truth; he used common images of agriculture, fishing, and family. Paul didn't use religious language to take the gospel to the Gentile world; he borrowed the legal terms of grace, sanctification, and justification from Roman culture. Often, the idea that transforms a discipline or shifts a paradigm is an idea that comes from the outside. Scientific breakthroughs frequently come as a result of laymen and laywomen stumbling upon them. Some of the major medical miracles discovered in the last century were the result of "accidents" outside the medical field.

It is human nature to see the world through filters (mental maps). When we continually cover familiar territory, we are blind to seeing new things. We may be unable to see what we do not expect to see. We shape reality to fit our existing paradigms. However, when we enter unfamiliar territory, we see many new things, and we process them differently. Reading information that is outside our areas of expertise pushes us to see things in a new way. Many of the most compelling theological arguments of this century have come about through the challenges of physics, mathematics, astronomy, and even cooking. Psychology, medicine, philosophy, and sociology all struggle with many of the same issues as the church. We can have our horizons broadened, our assumptions challenged, and our paradigm awareness enlarged by reading books, magazines, and journals that take us to new fields of information.

The same is true of movies and television. Modern parables are played out on screens both large and small every day. Millions of people are watching movies, videos, and television right this minute. Their view of the world is being shaped, and they are encountering thousands of stories each week. We need to be aware of the cultural images that emerge from and shape our paradigms. We cannot respond to that which we ignore, deny, or are unaware of. Paradigm thinkers are open to ideas and images, and they seek ways to bridge the secular and the sacred.

Too often, we fall into the trap of judging books, movies, television, and magazines as secular, worldly, and therefore inappropriate for use within the church. We do the same thing with business language, educational concepts, and science terms when applied to the church. But our biblical tradition teaches us to use the language and images of the culture. The secular/sacred distinction is mostly artificial. God works all things together for good. Paradigm thinkers are constantly amazed at the myriad ways God reveals good news in the world.

Find Success in Every Attempt

It is dangerous to measure every act in terms of success or failure. We figure, "Success is good, failure is not." The flaw in this reasoning is that there is usually more to learn from failure than from success. If we are committed to learning and improving, then there is no such thing as failure. Every attempt we make is an opportunity for growth, development, and learning. Paradigm thinkers understand that there is much to be gained from every risk. When we are punished for our failures, we are less likely to try new things. When we seek success in every attempt, and when we measure any learning as success, then we never fail. We are encouraged to try, and we continuously improve. This is a wonderful cycle to set in motion.

Paradigm thinking is a commitment to see the world from a systems perspective. It is a big-picture, long-view approach to reality. It sees each situation as a multifaceted gemstone. To know the full beauty and value of the stone, one must view it from all sides. To gain the greatest benefit from life, one must view it from all sides as well. When we develop this ability, we become more flexible. We can respond to shifting paradigms and change, and we are better prepared to minister to the people we serve.

It is interesting to note that Paul was indeed a paradigm thinker. He was always ready to challenge assumptions, explore alternatives, and utilize other points of view. He saw every experience, good or bad, as an opportunity to bring God's message to the people around him. Embracing change helped Paul to mature along his faith journey.

Questions for Discussion

In what ways do the apostles model paradigm thinking in the Book of Acts? How does Peter enable the Jerusalem leadership to understand the changing (Gentile) paradigm?

How do we make our congregations "change ready"? How can we help members of our fellowship adopt paradigm thinking that will promote spiritual growth and development?

_____

_____

_____

_____

Session 8: The Road to Transformation

Discovery
Naming Our Current Reality

In the church, we have many processes that align to enable the mission of making disciples of Jesus Christ. Paradigm thinking makes it possible to improve each process in a variety of ways. It is important to remember that processes can be improved only to a limited degree in the wrong system. A good system can be improved continuously. When paradigm thinking is applied as a way of "fixing" or "tinkering with" a poor system, then there is no real improvement. With the right system, such thinking allows us to see endless possibilities for development and improvement.

Exercise

How does an understanding of "quality" and "focus on the customer," as discussed in Sessions 7 and 8, help us to improve in a faith-forming-community paradigm? How might the ideas of "quality" and "focus on the customer" be applied to the practice of the spiritual disciplines (the means of grace)? For example, how might the quality of your celebration of the Lord's Supper be improved? You can ask a similar question about each means of grace in Figure 8A and talk about your insights with the whole group.

For Resources, Teaching Aids, and Newest Information

Check out our website at www.faithquest.net.

Figure 8A

A circular diagram with arrows pointing clockwise, labeled "Quality & Customers" in the center, surrounded by: Study of Scripture, Visiting the Sick, Service, Fasting, Prayer, Acts of Mercy, Lord's Supper, Christian Conference.

73

SESSION 9:
Called to Serve

Scriptures:
- Acts 13:1–19:19
  Focus Verses: Acts 14:1-28

Key Biblical Concepts:
- Different leadership styles for different missionary frontiers
- Enthusiasm and excitement in the early days of the Christian faith
- Power in the early church

Key Concepts for the Journey:
- Leadership styles
- The need for teams

Outline:
- Gathering
- A Time of Centering
- Prayer
- Preparation
  Questions and Answers
- Exploration
  A Reflective Moment Along the Way
  Questions and Small-Group Exercises
- Discovery
- Conclusion

Introduction

The mission of the Way (the early name given by outsiders to the Christian movement) spread in two distinct directions: (1) to the Jewish converts who saw Christ as the fulfillment of their Messianic anticipation and (2) to the Gentiles who were welcomed and received as God's people for the very first time. The story in Acts moves from the Jewish mission of the apostles to the missionary journeys of Paul and the spread of Christianity worldwide.

Prayer

Most holy God, help us to see the church as you see it. Instead of limiting our vision to what we know and are comfortable with, enable us to see the church in its full potential. Rather than claiming the church to be our own, let us proclaim the church as yours, open to all who will come. Make us a new church, that we might participate in the salvation of new people, in new places, in a new time. We pray in the name of Jesus, the Christ. Amen.

Preparation
Daily Scripture References and Questions for Reflection

Day 1 — Acts 13:1-52

How does Paul's message of salvation differ from the messages of Jesus and Peter? How does audience response to Paul's message differ from the usual response to the messages of Jesus or Peter? Why?

_____

_____

_____

_____

_____

_____

Day 2 — Acts 14:1-28
Why do you think the unbelieving Jews were so effective at turning the crowds against Paul? In what ways does the initial fervor with which Paul and Barnabas are received in new places bring to mind Jesus' triumphal entry into Jerusalem?

Day 3 — Acts 15:36–16:40
What do Paul and Silas do to earn imprisonment in Philippi? What reasons, other than religious, motivate people to reject the Christian faith?

Day 4 — Acts 17:1–18:23
What does it mean to be "religious" (17:22)? How is being "Christian" different from being "religious"?

Day 5 — Acts 18:24–19:19
How do the Christian leaders in Ephesus respond to Apollos? What differentiates Apollos and Paul from the Sons of Sceva?

Day 6
Read the session material and make notes in the margins.

Exploration
Background Information: Different Leadership Styles for Different Missionary Frontiers

What would have happened to the Christian movement if there had never been a Paul? Much of our theology, our organization, our sense of mission, our understanding of the saving work of Jesus Christ, and our core values emerge from the writings of Paul. Were we to erase the stories about Paul in the Book of Acts and all of the writings ascribed to the apostle Paul, we would find ourselves practicing a radically different faith and relating to a distinctly different Jesus Christ. The thinking and teaching of Paul so infuses Christianity that we may not be able to see how fundamentally our understanding of God in Jesus Christ is Pauline. We are as much a Pauline church as we are a Christian church.

Since Jesus called twelve disciples to teach, to train, and to test, and since he spent three years living and working with them, why did he call another from outside to take on the largest task of all? As the disciples adopted the mantle of apostleship, moving forth into the world, why did it not fall to one of them to become the apostle to the Gentiles? Peter even claims that role first in Acts. But history proves that it was Paul who was the apostle to the Gentiles, and it was through Paul's missionary efforts that the seeds were planted for the Christian church. Paul shattered the provincial confines of the Way and transformed the Christian movement into a cosmopolitan marvel. While Paul's personal influence waned, the momentum of Paul's teaching consistently increased. Paul accomplished what no other person could. Paul was called by God and empowered by the Holy Spirit to take the gospel of Jesus Christ to the Gentile world.

Paul was a different kind of leader from any of the Twelve. The Book of Acts repeatedly reports the benefit to Paul of being born a Roman citizen—a claim none of the other apostles could make. Paul was trained as a Pharisee and educated as a Roman citizen. He understood both the Law of Moses and the law of the Roman Empire. He was versed in Greek culture, art, music, and drama. Paul understood the political systems of his time, and he was experienced in ways that the other apostles were not.

Additionally, Paul possessed a single-minded drive to accomplish his task. He applied logical thought, sound planning, powerful rhetoric, and undaunted courage to the task of spreading the good news. He was a driven individual who used his forceful personality to full effect. Unlike Peter—who often acted first, then considered the consequences—Paul operated strategically, deliberately, and precisely. The original twelve disciples would have found themselves strangers in a strange land as they moved through Asia Minor into Rome and beyond to Europe. Paul found himself at home in those settings. It is God's wisdom that we should not only use our gifts and talents wisely, but that we should use them in settings most appropriate, where the benefits are destined to be most successful.

Enthusiasm for the Good News

It is refreshing to read the accounts where the gospel message that Paul delivered was so readily and enthusiastically received. It is disheartening, though, to note how often the religious leaders turned the crowds against Paul and his message and Paul was beaten, flogged, or stoned. The author of Luke and Acts reports a common quirk of human nature that often arises in the presence of charismatic leadership: fickleness. To be fickle is to lack steadfastness, to change one's opinion often. When Jesus entered Jerusalem riding on a mule, the crowds shouted, "Hosanna!" and proclaimed him king. One week later, many of those people called for his crucifixion. In the heat of the moment, they were swept up in heady enthusiasm. When the moment passed, they lost their sense of excitement and looked for the next emotional wave to ride.

This phenomenon plagued Paul at every turn. Paul would enter a new area and share the good news of Jesus Christ. He shared his story of conversion and redemption, and the people were enthralled. They begged to hear more; and they heralded Paul as apostle, prophet, even god. Then, someone would come along who argued against Paul and incited the crowd. Those who adored him one day, beat and ridiculed him the next.

In the face of this kind of behavior, it is amazing that Paul stayed committed to his task. Yet it is exactly this kind of behavior that Christ came into the world to heal. Historically, it has been the inability of human beings to hold fast to the promises of God that has resulted in broken covenants. The "enthusiasm"—the in-breathing of God into our hearts—dissipates and we lose faith. The author of Luke and Acts is clear that there is but one remedy for this human fickleness, and that is the baptism of the Holy Spirit. To be Spirit-filled is to be "enthused." Once the Spirit descends fully upon us, we never lose heart, we never flag in our steadfastness. The survival of the church depends upon the presence of the Holy Spirit. When the Spirit descends, transformation occurs.

The Holy Spirit of God strengthened Paul and the other apostles to continue to proclaim the gospel to a fickle world. The Holy Spirit empowers the church to pursue its mission, regardless of the reception the church receives. The Spirit of God cares little for popularity in the world. The Spirit exists within the church to sustain it and to provide the foundation upon which the kingdom of God might be built. This Spirit-based enthusiasm was the source of incredible power in the primitive Christian church.

Power in the Early Church

The Book of Acts is filled with wondrous stories of the power of God. Persecutors are converted, dead people rise, prisons burst open, healing and miracles abound, and heretics are struck dead. These mighty acts of power incite conversion and commitment, but they are secondary to the power and authority of the good news. It is in the teaching and in the charisma of the early church leaders that the real power rests. Through the empowerment of the Holy Spirit, ordinary men and women perform extraordinary acts.

The Book of Acts regularly refers to magicians, diviners of mystical knowledge, exorcists, and wielders of worldly power. These people were greatly revered and feared in their day. The supernatural character of their power set them apart. Peter and Paul moved into a cultural sphere that respected the mystic arts. It would have been easy for the apostles to have competed with the supernatural leaders to prove the superiority of God. However, that was not the arena in which they chose to compete. Paul, especially, employed persuasion and reason to make his case for salvation in Christ. The power of the early church lay within its spiritual center. It was not through magic, overt acts of power, or healing miracles that the truth of Christ emerged. The Christian church was built upon the faithful witness of men and women whose lives were changed. It is upon that foundation that the church remains to this day. Ours is not a faith of flash and fancy, but a rock-solid faith built upon the power of God to change lives.

A Reflective Moment Along the Way

How does the contemporary search for spirituality challenge today's church? What can the church learn from listening to this need being expressed? How is it similar to or different from the challenges faced by Paul's ministry?

When you meet together, talk about your responses. Then, sing or read in unison "The Church's One Foundation." In what ways does this hymn prayerfully consider the challenges to the church today? Talk about your thoughts as a group.

Key Concepts for the Journey
Leadership Styles

There has been a surge of books written on leadership in the past forty years. On average, a dozen new titles appear each month, offering surefire tips on how to be an effective leader. Leadership styles change, move in and out of fashion, and compete; but one thing is certain: no one style is right for everyone. In fact, no one style is the right style. The manner in which we lead will be effective sometimes, ineffective at other times. Our style of leadership will work with some people, and it will fail with others. We will share similar styles with some leaders, and we will be at odds with other leaders. Our leadership style is unique to us and reflects who we are, what we believe, and how we define our mission.

Some say that leadership style is determined by personality. Others say that leadership style is what we adopt to get things done. Still others claim that there is no such thing as leadership "style," but that we are who we are and leadership is something we do. The truth lies somewhere in the middle of these three positions.

People approach tasks differently. Some people are happy to step out of the way and let others lead. God creates followers, too. Effective followers are key to effective leadership. One valid leadership style is to not lead at all. We can identify four basic styles of leadership that most people employ: the thinker, the director, the pleaser, and the dreamer.[6]

The Thinker

The thinker is logical, precise, cautious, highly organized, methodical, laid-back, unemotional, quiet, deliberate, and prone to worry. The thinker stays out of the spotlight (leads from behind the scenes). He or she is task-oriented, single-minded, and likes lots of paper (memos, budgets, agendas, reports).

The Director

The director is direct, intense, focused, precise, forceful, opinionated, fast-talking, fast-acting, risk-taking, decisive, and time-conscious. He or she is up-front and in the spotlight, task-oriented and outspoken. The director wants results now, expects top performance from others, and is impatient.

The Pleaser

The pleaser is enthusiastic, considerate, fair, somewhat laid-back, and informal. He or she prefers teamwork to individual effort, is conscious of details, and is a good listener. The pleaser leads from the sidelines and enables others to perform and succeed. He or she is people-oriented and hard working, and the pleaser works alongside the rest of the group.

The Dreamer

The dreamer is creative, energetic, outspoken, fun-loving, disorganized, artistic, visual, risk-taking, loud, intense, tireless, and always ready for action. The dreamer loves the spotlight, loves people, likes more than one project at a time, and is always looking to the future. The dreamer is not bothered by details.

Each of these leadership types is a mere sketch of the qualities involved in leadership. Every person in leadership functions in all four roles from time to time, but there usually is one dominant style. All four styles are valid and equally valuable. Each works best in specific situations. No style is appropriate for every task. Effective leadership is really a corporate act. Truly powerful leadership will take place only in teams where all four styles are well-represented. One person will not be effective in all four styles; however, a number of people will more than likely encompass a greater span of styles and skills.

The apostle Paul was a director. Peter was a dreamer; Thomas, a thinker; Philip, a pleaser. Think of other characters from Scripture. Based on these thumbnail descriptions, where might you put Mary and Martha, Judas, Mary Magdalene, Moses, Elijah, John the Baptist, Abraham, David, Ruth, or others? Reflect on the different stories of Jesus and see how he moved from one style to another as the situation dictated. The Bible clearly reflects these four styles of leadership, and it offers us models for ways to employ these styles to fulfill the mission of the church effectively.

The Need for Teams

In a Metropolitan church, two pastors were at war. The senior pastor was a quiet, methodical man who wanted to establish a stable, peaceful faith community. The associate pastor was a woman who had a vision for a church that served the community as a center for justice and social action. She was an energetic, passionate, and deeply spiritual leader. The two pastors spent as much time trying to convert each other and their congregation as they did actually sharing in the ministry. Instead of finding a way to work together, they drove each other crazy.

This is not an unusual tale. Different styles often don't mix. The reason is simple: Too often we assume that our style is the right style and that anyone who does things differently does so out of ignorance. Then it becomes our job to fix that person.

Leadership styles are not right or wrong; they are just different. One style might not be appropriate to a specific situation, but that doesn't make it wrong. However, most organizations require a wide variety of gifts and skills to run efficiently. Effective organizations require team leadership.

Team was a buzzword of the 1990's. It can mean many things, and it has become so overused that almost any group of people is referred to as a team. For our purposes, we will use Jon Katzenbach and Douglas Smith's definition of *team*: "a small number of people with complementary skills who are committed to a common purpose, performance goals, and approach for which they hold themselves mutually accountable."[7] This definition helps us understand what makes teams unique and how they might be relevant for maximizing the effectiveness of a congregation's leadership. First, teams are composed of "a small number of people." They operate best with five to eight members. This size allows flexibility and ease of scheduling work and time together. Moreover, it is a manageable size.

Second, team members have "complementary skills." Effective teams rarely self-select. Teams are "built" around the skills and abilities needed to accomplish a task. Individuals are brought together so that their combined strengths might compensate for any weakness. When each team member brings unique skills and knowledge to a project, the result is synergy. (Synergy is that state in which the total effect is greater than the sum of the parts. The biblical metaphor of the body of Christ illustrates synergy.) True teams are designed to be synergistic.

Third, team members are "committed to a common purpose." They are aligned around the mission of the organization. When a team has clarity about mission, vision, and aim, then it can function effectively. With a common purpose, everyone draws energy from the same source, and the team's energy is channeled toward the same outcome. Common purpose is vital to keep teams focused and cohesive.

Fourth, teams are defined by "performance goals." This important distinction is frequently overlooked. A team exists to accomplish a certain task or a set of tasks. The team, therefore, has a clear performance objective. Once that objective is reached, the team disbands. This is a critical area in which teams differ from committees, boards, or work groups. The function of a team is clearly defined, and the progress of a team is easily measurable.

Fifth, teams design and share an "approach" or method for getting work done. One seminal function of every team is to decide how members will work together: who is responsible for what, where are the lines of authority and accountability, what is the time frame, and how will the work be evaluated? Team members answer these questions together. The team is an autonomous group that works together to maximize effectiveness. If standards and practices are imposed from outside or above, then a team doesn't really exist.

Finally, teams "hold themselves mutually accountable." Teams need to be free to make their own decisions, take their own risks, and make necessary changes and modifications without the laborious constraint of reporting progress to a parent group. Teams are entrusted with the faith of the organization that they will serve the best interests of the greater whole. Since the team is designed around a task that is aligned with the mission and vision of the organization, this shouldn't be a problem. People sometimes fear that teams will exploit their freedom. In organizations where there is a low level of trust, teams are probably not going to work. Teams must hold themselves accountable, and they must continuously yield a level of quality output that justifies their autonomy.

It is fairly easy to see how teams differ from committees in the church. There are drawbacks to committee-based systems—in the way we experience them. First, committees rarely have clearly defined performance objectives. Many committee members lack clarity about what they are supposed to do.

Second, committees tend to be too large to be effective. They include a lot of people—and therefore reflect a large opinion base—but many of these people feel incidental to the real work being done. Often the processes get slowed to ensure that everyone is heard.

Third, evaluation processes tend to be sloppy. In many cases, there is no evaluation process to measure the committee's effectiveness.

Finally, committees tend to have a large amount of work, and agendas become cumbersome. The work of the committee then becomes getting through the agenda instead of dealing with what is on the agenda. Over time, many committees become ends in themselves instead of means to the end of fulfilling the mission of making disciples of Jesus Christ.

In our churches, leaders come bearing a variety of skills and knowledge, experience and wisdom, and leadership styles. The organizational structure of the congregation should optimize these diverse human resources. This is a key act of stewardship as it will be discussed in Session 14. How we manage the gifts we have been given by God—especially human gifts—is the very definition of stewardship. It is poor stewardship to underuse the leadership potential in our congregations. By learning to affirm and support different leadership styles and by moving from committee-based ministries to team-based ministries, we can dramatically improve our systems for congregational leadership and maximize the potential of men and women who faithfully answer the call to serve.

Questions for Discussion

How are the leadership styles of Jesus, Peter, and Paul different? In what ways do the disciples/apostles model team leadership?

Talk about the experiences you have had in being part of a team. In what ways do you experience team leadership in your congregation? Where do you witness good models of team leadership today?

_____

_____

_____

_____

_____

Discovery
Naming Our Current Reality

Developing faith-forming communities requires leaders who understand the benefits of team-based ministry, who honor and identify a wide variety of gifts, and who create systems for continuous learning and improvement. Faith-forming communities celebrate diversity; they need leaders who reflect the various styles and approaches to leadership.

Referring to the four leadership styles named on pages 78-79, what is your predominant style? Do others in the group agree? Why or why not?

What is the dominant leadership style in your group? Is it representative of the dominant leadership style of your congregation?

In what ways does your church use each of the four basic styles? Are any styles less well represented than others?

Exercise

Look at the church-related tasks in Figure 9A. The first column lists tasks that might be part of a faith-forming-community. What gifts, knowledge, skills, and leadership styles would you look for to create effective teams to work on these tasks?

For Resources, Teaching Aids, and Newest Information

Check out our website at www.faithquest.net.

Figure 9A

TASKS	GIFTS	KNOWLEDGE	SKILLS	LEADERSHIP STYLE
The development of a contemporary worship service				
A new visitation program for newcomers to the community				
A capital-funds campaign to build a new sanctuary				
A literacy program for teaching adults and children in the inner city				

SESSION 10:
To the Ends of the Earth

Scriptures:
- Acts 19:21–20:38; 21:37–28:31
  Focus Verses: Acts 28:17-31

Key Biblical Concepts:
- Personal testimony
- Experiencing the presence of God
- There are no gray areas in the gospel

Key Concepts for the Journey:
- Chaos theory
- Juggling and mastering the art of life

Outline:
- Gathering
- A Time of Centering
- Prayer
- Preparation
  Questions and Answers
- Exploration
  A Reflective Moment Along the Way
  Questions and Small-Group Exercises
- Discovery
- Conclusion

Introduction

The early Christian movement faced incredible opposition and persecution. It was often life-threatening to profess belief in Jesus Christ as the Son of God. Everywhere that the apostles took the message of Christ raised from the dead, they met resistance. The development of authentic Christian community required sacrifice of security, family, tradition, and safety. Judaism provided an anchor in a chaotic world. Breaking ties with the Hebrew faith cast Christian converts into the maelstrom. Early Christians embraced chaos, and they found a new, marvelous order.

Prayer

From chaos, you bring order, O God. From nothingness, you bring light and life. Help us to put our trust in you; to have confidence that throughout all the storms of life, you will keep us safe. As we face the turbulent times of life, grant us, by the power of your Holy Spirit, the courage to live in the light of your grace and to share the good news with others. Amen.

Preparation
Daily Scripture References and Questions for Reflection

Day 1 — Acts 19:21–20:6
How do the opposing religious groups address their differences? What secular issues influenced the disputes among these groups?

_____
_____
_____
_____
_____
_____
_____

FaithQuest: A New Way of Thinking About the Church

Day 2 — Acts 20:7-38

Isn't it comforting to know that there is a biblical precedent for falling asleep during the sermon? What does Paul mean when he describes himself as a "captive to the Spirit"?

_____
_____
_____
_____
_____
_____

Day 3 — Acts 21:37-24:27

Why are the officials in Jerusalem outraged by Paul's testimony (Acts 22:22)?

_____
_____
_____
_____
_____
_____

Day 4 — Acts 25:1-26:32

Why do Paul's religious opponents attempt to get the Roman legal system to take care of Paul for them? How do Festus and King Agrippa react to Paul's testimony?

_____
_____
_____
_____
_____

Day 5 — Acts 27:1-28:31

How do the final words of Paul echo those of Jesus in the Gospel of Luke? In what ways are the two sets of parting words different?

_____
_____
_____
_____
_____
_____

Day 6

Read the session material and make notes in the margins.

Exploration
Background Information: Personal Testimony

Jesus came proclaiming the kingdom of God, offering salvation to any who would repent and be baptized. He taught in parables and metaphor, and he built upon the Law and the Prophets to establish a new paradigm. Jesus rarely referred to his own life story as a way to prove any of his claims.

Paul had a story to tell. It was a powerful account of how Jesus Christ changes lives. The power of Paul's preaching lay within his personal testimony. He recounted how he began life persecuting the followers of the Way, then experienced conversion on the road to Damascus as he encountered the risen Christ, and finally how he was empowered by the Holy Spirit of God to preach good news to the Gentiles, standing up to torture, ridicule, and threat of death. Those who knew Saul in his former life could not deny the impressive power that had changed his life.

The power of the gospel was not in being able to say the things that Jesus said or to do the things that Jesus did or to preach, pray, or prophesy mightily. The power of the gospel lay in the testimony of witnesses to the power of Jesus Christ. The men and women who changed the world and established the Christian church did so by telling their own stories: the stories of what Jesus did in their lives.

The mission of the church—making disciples of Jesus Christ—is all about changing lives. Changed lives change the world. The most powerful way to change lives is to introduce people to the power that transforms. The best way to communicate that power is to speak from personal experience.

If we take our call to make disciples seriously, we need to create opportunities that allow people to share their stories. When we get serious about listening to the people we serve, we will find that we have made sacred space for those stories to be shared and heard.

Experiencing the Presence of God

Paul lived with an assurance that is astounding. He was able to face perils and problems that would turn back the heartiest souls. He spoke with conviction in front of audiences of powerful men who held his fate in their hands. He challenged authority in the fine tradition of Jesus Christ, and he refused to compromise his message and mission for anyone. His was an impressive example of courage, commitment, and faith.

Paul experienced a real and intimate presence of Christ. This immanence of Christ enabled Paul to move through the world as a new kind of man. His conversion was a conversion not merely of faith but of life. In Christ, Paul lived a new way. This new way is open to all who accept Christ as Savior and Lord.

The church exists to provide that place where people can come to experience the presence of God. In a world of chaos, peril, and potential danger, the church stands as a way station, where God's order reigns. The mission of making disciples is the end result of the primary task of reaching out and receiving people in Christ, relating them to God, nurturing and strengthening them in the faith, and sending them forth into chaos to live ordered, balanced lives. This core process will not work unless people encounter the presence of God. Once people's lives are truly touched by God's presence, they are empowered to live faithfully as Christian disciples.

A New Way of Understanding Life

In the Book of Acts, there are no halfway Christians. Christian faith was a life-and-death matter; and a person either believed or didn't. Belief was an active practice, and people's lives reflected what they truly felt. To accept Jesus Christ was to cut all ties with the former religious community. Wherever the apostles took the gospel of Jesus Christ, people made a clear decision whether to accept or to reject it. Acceptance meant a total change of life. Rejection came in a variety of ways. Some debated the truth of the gospel, while others questioned the sanity of the apostles. Still others simply ignored the gospel altogether. The only option not available was to adopt a passive Christian faith, where lifestyle remained unaffected.

Passive Christianity is problematic. A belief system that doesn't alter behavior is worthless. Deeply held values shape behavior, whether individual or corporate. When values change, behavior changes. The church is a spiritual center based on values defined by Christ. When we invite people to join the community of faith, we invite them to accept the core values of the community; and that requires change. By God's grace, transformation occurs. The process of making disciples is a process of changing lives and shaping values. People who enter a Christian community will move forth from that community as changed people. It is imperative that the Christian church of the twenty-first century attend to changing lives.

A Reflective Moment Along the Way

John Wesley organized a system for discipleship that included the Class Meeting. A small group of people committed to growing in their relationship with Christ met together weekly and found a life-changing power in the sharing of their struggles, their brokenness, and their joys. If one member of the group needed help changing some segment of his or her life, the whole group supported that person in love as they held one another accountable.

Think of a time when someone's spiritual strength or personal story helped you in a time of personal need. In what setting was that witness experienced? End the time by entering into three minutes of silent prayer thanking God for the witness of those people in your lives.

Key Concepts for the Journey
Chaos Theory

Look back at the prayer at the beginning of this session. It is evident from the first page of the Bible that God creates by molding chaos. From the chaos of a dark and turbulent world came the ordering of creation, and God saw that "it was good"!

When the Israelites were set free from captivity through the Exodus, the scene was a mad explosion of chaos. People gathering belongings, carrying food and water, leading children and animals. Think about the chaos of the darkness that made the escape even more difficult. Can you imagine the cries of the wailing parents discovering the visitation of the angel of death upon their children? All this was followed by the utter rage of Pharaoh as his army chased the fleeing slaves, then the miracle of the parting of the waters, and the drowning of Pharaoh's proudest and best. Later in the story the wilderness became the next adventure along the journey of faith with all of its chaotic moments. Yet, out of all of this chaos came the birth of a new day for the people of God.

The persecution of the church in the Book of Acts clearly exemplifies what it means to experience the cost of discipleship. To be thrust into the uncertainty and risk of choosing the Christian life called for not only a great depth of faith but also the ability to take on all that life could hand them and still remain firmly anchored in Christ.

In our world that seems to be so full of chaos, it is only natural to seek a sense of balance and order. Broken relationships, the threat of terrorism, a fluctuating economy, the challenge of raising children in an increasingly hostile environment, the plight of the poor and hungry, make us ask how we can remain faithful in the midst of it all. How can we live with a blessed assurance that God is the victor of everything and of every age?

We can look at modern chaos theory for some helpful clues. Chaos theory states that chaos is only apparent and that underlying the seeming randomness in the world is a wonderfully complex, highly-ordered reality.[8] Chaos exists due to our limited ability to comprehend the enormity of life. Chaos is a good thing, contrary to popular consensus.

Chaos theory encourages us to stop trying so hard to create order. It invites us, instead, to turn our attention to discovering the order inherent in nature. A fundamental tenet of chaos theory is that organisms will self-organize, given enough time and space. Imposing artificial organizational structures is not the way to combat chaos. Such structures may actually contribute to chaos.

Chaos theory suggests that disorder is a matter more of perception than of reality. We experience chaos because we lack understanding. As we deepen our learning and comprehend more of the complexity of nature, life becomes less chaotic. Organisms tend toward self-organization to build connection and control over their environment.

An organization develops its own structure as a way to control its environment and to build connection. In human structures, relationship-building creates community and gives people a sense of control over their environments. Community results when people focus on people instead of on the organization. An organizational structure should be a means to an end. For instance, envisioning a need, those people set free from structure will discover a way to meet the need, eventually building a support system around the vision. This action is sometimes referred to in other arenas as "form following function." In the church, the structure should facilitate relationship-building. If the structure becomes an end in itself—existing merely to have meetings and elect new participants—it loses its power to combat chaos. Where relationships are strong, chaos abates.

The current reality of many congregations is that they employ the wrong organizational structure to fulfill the mission of the church. The organizational design most commonly used is fifty years old. The church's organizational structure was transferred from corporate America, with minutes, agendas, *Robert's Rules of Order*, timekeepers, and committee reports. Although the structure may have worked better when it was first developed—which many people question—it certainly is not valid today.

The times have changed, and the need for structure has changed as well. In 1996, The United Methodist Church acknowledged this need by "deconstructing" the organizational recommendations in the *Book of Discipline*. It gave local congregations liberal latitude to design structures appropriate to their needs. Local churches were encouraged to do what works instead of what is required.

Out of the chaos of elaborate structures and cumbersome committees there are emerging self-organizing systems for ministry. People are amazed when they discover that there are alternative ways to work. Teams provide energy and impetus to get things done. Congregational planning sessions replace councils on ministry, and a new generation of church leaders is emerging. Streamlined committees discover that fewer people can accomplish more. Clergy and laity alike report less burnout and frustration since the burden of "filling slots" in the leadership hierarchy has been lifted. Worship still happens in the absence of a formal worship committee. People still give money in the absence of formal commitment campaigns. Children are still educated and affirmed in the absence of large Christian education committees. All the vital work of the church continues as new and more effective methods of leadership arrive. Out of the randomness and uncertainty of human interpersonal dynamics, order issues forth.

But what about our lives? If chaos is part of God's creative ordering, how are we to live with a sense of security? How can we handle all the challenges that come our way and still live faithful, balanced lives? What follows are some helpful tools.

Juggling and Mastering the Art of Life

Order appears out of chaos for organisms, but what about for individuals? How do we find order amidst the chaos in our individual lives? Michael Gelb and Tony Buzan offer a helpful metaphor in their engaging book *Lessons From the Art of Juggling*.[9]

To master the art of juggling, one must have balance, poise, rhythm, and playfulness. Aren't these also the essential abilities for mastering the art of life? Look at Figure 10A and think about your own life. What are you trying to juggle?

Balance

A regular feature on the old *Ed Sullivan Show* was a man who would set a dozen plates spinning atop a dozen willowy poles. He would race from pole to pole as the plates began to slow down and wobble. This plate juggler looked absolutely frantic as he attempted to keep all his plates spinning at once. The image is appropriate for many of us who juggle a variety of demands. When racing from "pole to pole," we find it difficult to feel balanced. Too often, we feel out of control. However, no one is going to make us feel balanced and in control. We must do that for ourselves.

Jesus offers a model of balance in a chaotic life. Amid all the confrontation and constant movement, Jesus regularly engaged in prayer and retreat. No matter how demanding the pressures, Jesus withdrew to pray. In prayer, Jesus centered himself in the power and presence of God, and he was empowered by God's Spirit to continue his work. Prayer is essential for balance in the Christian life.

Praying, reading Scripture, and taking time for personal reflection are important elements in our faith formation and development as Christian disciples. We must protect time for these elements. If we desire balance in our lives, we must take steps to restore it. Our personal disciplines are the foundation upon which we establish balance.

Poise

A young woman led a group of four- and five-year-olds through a museum. The children chattered,

Figure 10A

ran in a thousand directions, pushed and pulled at one another, screamed, laughed, cried, and generally acted like children. The woman smiled and chatted with the children, herded them through the displays, stopped to comfort the distressed, and pointed out sights of interest. She displayed striking calm and poise. She was in her element with children, and the joy she felt in their presence was evident. Her sense of calm came from a deep internal source, and the children benefited from her warmth and devotion.

Poise is grace under fire. Poise is the ability to maintain balance throughout the storms of life. When we establish balance in our lives, we are able to stand up better to problems and pressures. When we are in close contact with our spiritual center, we have a deep well from which to draw. Poise allows us to keep our heads so that we can make wise, sensible decisions at critical times.

Once again, if we desire poise, we must take responsibility for developing it. To carry calm with us through the day, we must experience calm on a regular basis. A time of personal devotion will provide the necessary oasis of calm. Spiritual centering is at the heart of personal mastery and improvement. Prayer, study of Scripture, and personal reflection are entry points to this calming center.

Rhythm

There is a wonderful scene in the Australian film *Strictly Ballroom*[10]—a movie about competitive ballroom dancing—in which the main character, Scott, is asked by his dance partner's grandmother, "Where do you feel the rhythm?" Scott, displaying his technical brilliance, pounds out a cadence with his feet. The grandmother stops him, admonishing him, and begins tapping out a rhythm over his heart and stomach. "Here!" she says. Scott begins to feel the rhythm emanating from a new center, and his dancing is transformed. No longer living "off-center," Scott dances as he has never danced before.

True rhythm allows us to live in a new way. When we are in sync with the natural rhythms of creation, we are in harmony. We experience order in the midst of chaos. While we anticipate rhythm in music, we often miss rhythm in life. Nature has incredible rhythms and patterns. Rhythms occur in relationships. Rhythms and patterns in our bodies regulate our lives and provide health. There are natural rhythms to life all around us. When we take time to observe and admire these rhythms, they transform us.

It is helpful to set a specific time and place for personal devotions. We can establish a pattern for centering our hearts and minds on Jesus Christ. Early morning and the end of day are natural points to withdraw and focus upon God. For some, the lunch hour works best. There is no optimal time. What is important is to establish the pattern and discipline. If we view our time of devotion as an appointed meeting with God, we will be better able to keep covenant.

Within our prayer and reflection, we will experience rhythm. Attending to the beat of the heart or to breathing is an excellent way of centering and calming down. Praying in rhythm with breathing has a beautiful, quieting effect. When we live out of a rhythmic center, we carry it with us throughout the day; and we discover it everywhere we go. We avoid situations that disturb our rhythm, and we embrace life experiences that harmonize with our rhythm. Balance, poise, and rhythm blend to grant us peace and harmony; and others notice.

Playfulness

Sadly, we sometimes confuse seriousness about our faith with stoicism. When we enter the sanctuary, we check our joy at the door. We can get so caught up in the gravity of the pressures and problems of life that we forget to smile.

Jesus, as serious and dedicated to his mission as he was, employed humor and irony in his teachings. One of the key elements of the parable is absurdity. Some of the epic humor has been lost through translation and a different cultural context, but Jesus employed an incisive playfulness in his teaching. Jesus had a great time humorously delivering serious, weighty truths.

Think for a moment. Would you rather spend time with someone cheerful and happy or someone impassive and morose? Would you rather laugh or cry? Would you rather experience life as a blessing or as a curse? These are simple choices. Most people want to enjoy life and to share joy and happiness with others.

Life is too short to take too seriously. Certainly, there are matters of grave importance, and there will be times of genuine sadness and grief; but for the most part, life is what we make of it. Happiness is not a feeling so much as it is a decision. We can commit ourselves to being cheerful and extending joy to others. We can wake up in the morning with a pledge to be part of the solution to the world's problems. We can adopt a playful attitude that enables us to see the good in life rather than the bad. Regardless of how we feel inside, we can emanate humor, hope, and goodwill. Instead of taking a reactive stance toward happiness, we can be proactive.

When we consciously extend a positive demeanor, we are more attractive to others. When we engage in the mission of making disciples of Jesus Christ, we will find the path easier if we have a positive attitude. When we display a joy in living, a hopefulness for the future, and a playful approach to each day, others will want to know our secret. When our relationship with Jesus Christ empowers us to live differently in the world, then we have a story to tell and a witness to share.

Balance, poise, rhythm, and playfulness are the key qualities that will transform us from bunglers to jugglers. The word "juggler" comes from the Latin *joculari*—to jest or to be a fool. Paul invites us to become "fools for the sake of Christ" (1 Corinthians 4:10). Let us be jugglers, so that the wisdom of God might be known in us. Let us strive for balance, poise, rhythm, and playfulness so that we might know order in a world of chaos and become true examples of the power and presence of Jesus Christ in our lives. As we align our lives toward the goal of being faithful Christian disciples, we are able to participate in the mission of making disciples through our community of faith.

Questions for Discussion

Does your existing structure for ministry bring order out of chaos? Do people feel that the existing structure makes optimal use of their time, talents, and gifts?

How does your church assist people in developing balance, poise, rhythm, and playfulness in their lives? What might you do to provide more opportunities for people to develop these qualities?

Discovery
Naming Our Current Reality

When we organize the church for ministry, we focus on one of two points: the structure itself or the people who make up the structure. If we focus on people, we will design systems that use their gifts and talents appropriately. If we focus on the structure, then we will select only those people who best fit into "slots." It is vitally important to remember that systems should serve people, not the other way around.

Margaret Wheatley's model of "self-organizing" systems helps clarify this point: "A self-organizing system reveals itself as structures of relationships, patterns of behaviors, habits of belief, methods for accomplishing work."[11] In an organization, structures, patterns, habits, and methods are all observable. We pay attention to what we can see, so we devote time and energy to *what* and *how* things get done. What is not as visible is the *why*. The *why* is the purpose of the organization that reflects the values, ideas, shared sense of identity, and the relationships of the people. This is illustrated in Figure 10B. The unseen foundation is the information, relationships, and identity that are the purpose of the organization. What we see is the structure, patterns and processes that evolve from the foundation.

To explain this model, Wheatley speaks in terms of "domains."[12] (See Figure 10C.) She says that you cannot create the correct structure, patterns, and processes until you have first attended to identity, relationships, and information.

Structure, processes, and patterns of behavior cannot precede the establishment of identity, relationships, and sharing of information if the organization is to have integrity. Identity clarifies who we are, what we believe (our core values), and our sense of purpose (mission). Relationships clarify how we work together, play together, and live together. Information refers to how we communicate; how we disseminate facts, feelings, and ideas; and how we learn. These domains overlap to create a definition of the organization. As the organization is defined, it then is ready to develop structures, processes, and patterns for performance. Structures draw lines of responsibility and accountability and clarify specific tasks and projects. Processes are developed to achieve tasks and perform projects. Patterns develop in the form of traditions, habits, and rituals.

Identity, relationships, and information reflect the *character* of the organization; structure, processes, and patterns reflect the *behavior* of the organization. What an organization *is* is not the same as what an organization *does*. However, in strong organizations, being and doing are indistinguishable because the character and behavior are so closely aligned.

In the church, we are first and foremost about God, and about people. Our core process is a people process. It enables us to discover our identity, build relationships, and share information. The organizational structure should serve this process. We should evaluate our structures, patterns, and processes to determine how well they facilitate the flow of information and the strengthening of relationships and how well they reflect the mission and core values of our identity. Too much time is spent on the *what* and *how* of the church without adequate attention to the *why* of the church.

Exercise

Looking at Wheatley's domains and their equivalent entities in the church (in Figure 10C), discuss

Figure 10B

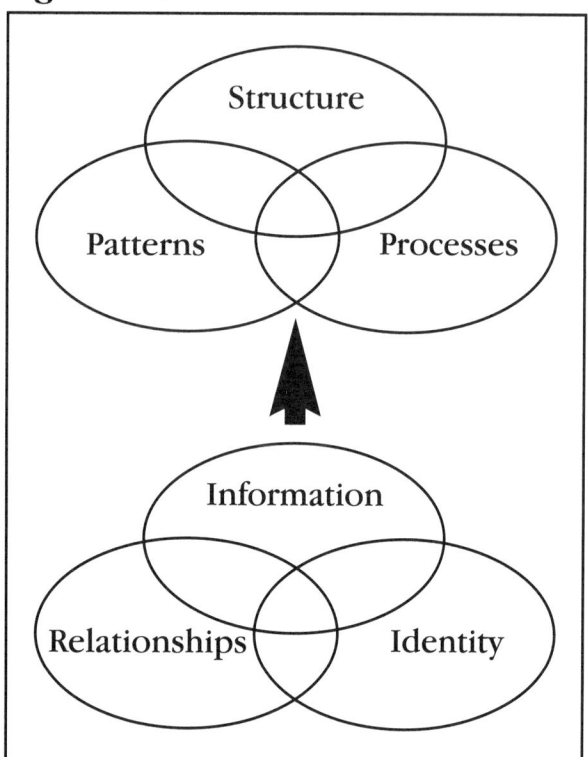

Figure 10C

DOMAIN	WHAT IS IN PLACE	WHAT IS NEEDED
Identity (Mission and core values)		
Relationships (Building community)		
Information (Sharing ideas; disseminating facts and feelings; how we learn)		
Structures (Organization for getting work done)		
Processes (The way we accomplish tasks and projects)		
Patterns (Habits, rituals, traditions that define how we do what we do)		

what is currently in place in your church to provide strength in each area. What could you do better in order to strengthen each domain? For example, how well do your members understand the core values of your church? Can they clearly state your mission? How could your church improve on your current understanding?

How does your church's structure reflect the mission, core values, and vision of the congregation? In what way is the current structure not faithful to the mission and core values?

The faith-forming-community paradigm demands that we revisit our understanding of mission, vision, values, and identity. As we clarify our identity in the post-Christendom era, what are the implications for developing structures, processes, and patterns that will help us respond to our changing world?

(Note: The two columns in Figure 10C could be changed to match the "activity center" and "faith-forming-community" models of churches. This exercise could help illustrate what the movement from one paradigm to the other might look like.)

Try this. Using Wheatley's theory of self-organizing structures, imagine your church without any programmatic committees! The need arises in the community for a ministry to the elderly. A shared vision has arisen suggesting that a weekly meal be offered free of charge to the community. On a sheet of newsprint, envision building a system of ministry to accomplish the goal. What support system would be needed to see the vision through? Is there a difference in designing the system after the vision is clear, as opposed to beginning with an organized structure or committee with a set of guidelines in place?

In what ways might your current local church structure actually impede God's use of chaos to bring about creation? Will the movement from the activity-center paradigm to the faith-forming paradigm bring about chaos in your congregation? What kind of response should we expect?

For Resources, Teaching Aids, and Newest Information

Check out our website at www.faithquest.net.

FAITH QUEST

SECTION 3
The Epistle to the Ephesians

A New Way of Thinking About the World

The letter to the Ephesians is the culmination of Pauline thought. In this short letter, the author presents a powerful vision for reconciliation and Christian living. A key word for this epistle is *union*. The letter to the Ephesians calls believers to union with God, union with Christ, union with brothers and sisters in the faith, and—surprisingly—union with strangers, enemies, and outcasts. The author of this letter moves readers beyond thinking within the confines of their immediate community to "A New Way of Thinking About the World."

SESSION 11:
Union With Christ

Scriptures:
- Ephesians 1:1–2:22
  Focus Verses: Ephesians 2:11-22

Key Biblical Concepts:
- Pauline theology
- Grace and justification by faith
- One universal church
- Reconciliation and unity

Key Concepts for the Journey:
- Three kinds of knowledge

Outline:
- Gathering
- A Time of Centering
- Prayer
- Preparation
  Questions and Answers
- Exploration
  A Reflective Moment Along the Way
  Questions and Small-Group Exercises
- Discovery
- Conclusion

Introduction

Ephesians is perhaps the best summary of Pauline theology presented in the New Testament. It incorporates the best features of Paul's thought and teaching, and it defines the identity of the church at the end of the first century. In this letter, we find guidance and instruction for being the church for the twenty-first century. There is a powerful "universal" picture of the church that applies as well today as it ever has. This session will help redefine the place of the church in the world.

Prayer

Gracious and merciful God, grant us the wisdom to see all creation through eyes of love and justice. Help us understand that the church is your gift to the entire world and that we are privileged to be a part of this amazing household of believers. Give us a vision for a worldwide church where the doors are open to everyone and where no one must stand outside. Teach us to love others as we are loved by you. We pray in Jesus' name. Amen.

Preparation
Daily Scripture References and Questions for Reflection

Day 1 — Ephesians 1:1–2:22
List any words, phrases, or ideas that catch your attention. What are the key points of these chapters?

_____
_____
_____
_____
_____
_____

Day 2 — Ephesians 1:1-14
Paul uses the phrase "in Christ" five times in these fourteen verses. What does this phrase mean to you?

_____
_____

FaithQuest: A New Way of Thinking About the World

Day 3 — Ephesians 1:15-23
What does Paul pray for in Ephesians 1:15-23? What is "the hope to which God has called you"?

Day 4 — Ephesians 2:1-10
What is the meaning of the phrase "by grace you have been saved" (verses 5, 8)? What is your understanding of "justification by faith"?

Day 5 — Ephesians 2:11-22
How has Christ "abolished the law"? (Compare with Luke 16:14-17.) Paul compares the church to the "household of God." In what ways is the church like a household?

Day 6
Read the session material and make notes in the margins.

Exploration
Background Information: Pauline Theology

The Book of Acts is about the apostle Paul, and the letter to the church at Ephesus is written in Paul's name. Letters written by other authors and ascribed to Paul are known as deutero-Pauline letters. This was a common practice in the time of Jesus and Paul. Students of a particular school of thought would carry on a tradition after the leader died by circulating letters in his (or her) name. There was no thought of deception or misrepresentation given to such practices; they were common and well accepted. The letter to the Ephesians, written toward the end of the first century (fully forty years after Paul's death), is contemporary with the writing of Luke and Acts. In Ephesians, we find a mature expression of Pauline theology.

The letter borrows many of its concepts and quotations from other, earlier letters. Fully one-third of Ephesians is drawn directly from Colossians. Of the 155 verses in Ephesians, 73 have verbal parallels in Colossians. There are also parallels with Romans, Galatians, and First and Second Corinthians.

Among the ideas central to the letter to the Ephesians are grace and justification by faith, one universal church and reconciliation of Jew and Gentile, and our becoming one with Christ.

Grace and Justification by Faith

No letter emphasizes the grace of Christ more powerfully than Ephesians. It is by grace that God saves us. No works are required, and no earthly effort will suffice—salvation comes as a freely given gift of God. We do not earn salvation; we do not deserve salvation; but we receive salvation, nonetheless. There is but one avenue to God's grace, and that is faith.

Faith justifies us in the eyes of God. Faith is our "yes" to the offer of salvation in Christ. Faith perfects us and opens us to the miraculous work of the Holy Spirit. Faith brings us "home" to God as prodigal sons and daughters, and grace is the "open arms" with which we are received. Nowhere does Paul offer a more loving, more affirming promise of acceptance and restoration.

One Reconciled Church

The vision of Jesus for the kingdom of God closely resembles Paul's vision for a universal church open to all people. God unconditionally accepts us and restores us to a new relationship with God and with each other. Salvation by grace through faith is the formula for Jew and Gentile, slave and free, male and female, circumcised and uncircumcised. In other writings, Paul uses words for the church that could apply equally well to a local congregation as to the universal church. In Ephesians, Paul uses only the Greek word *ekklesia* to refer to the universal church.

The image of the church is an all-inclusive, global body of believers who form a family of God and a household of faith. There is equity and openness. Earthly divisions disappear, and diverse people are brought together. Dividing walls of hostility are destroyed, and unity abides. The focal point for this new unity is Jesus the Christ. Christ is no longer the person of Jesus, and the cross of Christ is no longer the focal point of Paul's teaching. Now, the church is joined "in Christ"; and together believers become the living body of Christ alive in the world.

One in Christ

In the Ephesian letter we read that as Christians we are bound physically, emotionally, spiritually, and metaphysically to the risen Christ. We are not merely joined together by our faith in Christ, we become one in Christ—mystically linked together as parts of one body. There is no longer any division between us. Christ is never apart from us. Through the Holy Spirit of God, we are joined inseparably with Christ.

This concept was a source of strength and courage as the church prepared to face some of its most severe persecution. The Christian community found that it became increasingly dangerous to profess belief in Jesus Christ. The concept of being one in and with Christ meant that no individual Christian or community ever stood alone. Not only did they stand with Christ, but they stood with all other believers, wherever they might be. One of the most impressive marks of the Christian believers in the second and third century was the courage with which they held to the faith and the strength with which they bore persecution.

The letter to the Ephesians paints a picture of a different kind of church—one not tied to a location or time. A risen and living Christ incarnate in the community of believers empowered the early church to move into the world.

The time is ripe to reclaim that vision of the church for today.

A Reflective Moment Along the Way

Take a few minutes to sketch a symbol or a picture of what it looks like for the members of your congregation to be "united in Christ." Reflect on this image for a few minutes, asking God to lead you.

Then draw a symbol or image that represents for you the relationship your church has with other Christian churches in your community. How are you joined together? How are you acting alone?

Show your pictures when your group meets together. Comment on why you drew what you drew. Did anything surprise your group? What can be learned?

Key Concepts for the Journey

The epistle to the Ephesians speaks in universal terms about being one with Christ. If there is any letter in the New Testament that encourages Christians to continuously grow spiritually, it is the letter to the Ephesians.

Prior to this letter, Paul spoke of the need to develop spiritually and to behave in a manner fitting the gospel. Paul presents a "big-picture" view of time, faith, inclusiveness, and relationships. He challenges us to think in larger, more expansive terms. Ephesians invites us to think about the church and the world in a new way.

Paul understood the Christian life as a constant upward spiral of growth. Improvement was always possible. He believed and expected this as part of our faith journey. John Wesley taught the same principles as he encouraged the people of his day to move on towards becoming perfect in love. If salvation was the moment of awareness of becoming one in Christ, sanctification, as Wesley called it, was a continual process of spiritual growth that never ended in this life.

Three Kinds of Knowledge

What do we know, and how do we know it? What is knowledge, anyway? Is it facts and data? Is it experience? Is it practical or theoretical? Do we know knowledge when we see it?

One root of the word *knowledge* means "to come to." We may come to awareness. We may come to certainty. We may come to answers—or maybe just to new questions. Regardless, "to come to" connotes movement; knowledge takes us places. Knowledge is essential for growth and improvement. What we do with knowledge is also important. Unless we integrate knowledge in some way, it does us no good. We "come to" nothing.

There are at least three kinds of knowledge: spiritual knowledge, professional knowledge, and improvement knowledge.

Spiritual Knowledge

Spiritual knowledge—the knowledge of emotion and intuition—is centered not in the head but in the heart. It arises through deep processes that often defy reason. We know God; we know love; we know hope; we know fear; we know beauty in ways that do not always make sense. Being swept away by a Mozart symphony, a Renoir painting, or a Dickens novel is not something we decide to do. We come to know and acknowledge many things at deep, transcendent levels. We may feel a calling for our lives or have a desire to try something new and different. We may feel an attraction to another person that we know is right, but we don't know why we know it.

Discernment occurs at this level of knowledge. This is where we hone our intuitive processes to search our feelings and hunches for guidance. In modern Western culture, this kind of knowledge has not received the kind of respect and attention it deserves. Entire courses are taught on how to develop professional or technical knowledge, but little is offered to help people develop their spiritual knowledge. However, effective leaders in business, education, science, and medicine report that the key to their success lies in attending to their feelings and trusting their hunches. We see spiritual knowledge modeled all the time, but most of us view it as inferior to rational, "left-brain" thought processes and knowledge.

Spiritual knowledge is developed at our spiritual center. God builds spiritual knowledge in the lives of Christian men and women. Unless we discipline ourselves to attend to the things of the spirit, we will deny ourselves the opportunity to nurture spiritual knowledge. Spiritual knowledge is the base upon which we build our lives. Without a firm foundation of spiritual knowledge, the technical and systems knowledge we attain will benefit us less.

Professional Knowledge

Professional knowledge (also referred to as technical knowledge) is a body of facts, data, and information that we learn in order to do our jobs better, to develop new skills and abilities, and to function effectively in the world. Through the increase of professional knowledge, we develop expertise in specific areas. This type of knowledge allows an individual to continue to grow in his or her career, vocation, or area of interest. Most commonly, professional knowledge takes the form of "book learning" or training. Professional knowledge is pursued most readily in a classroom.

Professional knowledge is perhaps the least ethereal of the three kinds of knowledge. It has less to do with feelings and more to do with cold, hard facts. It is not intuitive but highly structured and rational. Although professional knowledge can be quite subjective, it is usually considered to be factual and reliable. Our modern Western culture values professional knowledge highly. Professional knowledge is closely associated with power, wealth, and success. As information becomes the currency of trade in today's world, professional knowledge may come to be even more highly valued. It is imperative that the people of God understand the interrelationship of the three kinds of knowledge and strive to keep them in proper balance.

Improvement Knowledge

What differentiates a coach from a player, a conductor from an orchestra member, or an effective manager from a worker? Fundamentally, it is the point of view. While a player focuses on his or her position, the coach must focus on how all the players work together. This is the traditional systems view.

Today, it is apparent that the systems view does not belong to the coach only; it should belong to players who see themselves as part of a system. Orchestra members who understand the interrelationships among all the different instruments rise to a new level of expertise. Workers who apply systems knowledge to their particular functional areas are more productive. The ability to see the larger picture and to use systems knowledge is key to breaking through to continuously improving performance.

Improvement knowledge (or systems knowledge) is often described as the ability to "walk the catwalk." As noted in an earlier session, catwalks over a factory floor allow managers and forepersons to oversee the entire production system. The ability to see the entire system enables leaders to make informed and accurate decisions.

Professional knowledge alone is not adequate for overseeing an entire system. Understanding interrelationships and making proper adjustments requires intuition and an ability to factor in all kinds of probabilities. Improvement knowledge requires a lot of experience and the ability to "play hunches." Improvement knowledge develops through trial and error, experimentation, and innovation. Improvement knowledge unleashes creativity and pioneering.

It is helpful to remember that—at one level—the three kinds of knowledge are artificial conceptual frames. Further, the three kinds of knowledge overlap. They are dynamically engaged rather than linear.

Often, we employ spiritual and professional knowledge to the exclusion of improvement knowledge. Without improvement knowledge, continuous improvement is impossible. The foundation of a true learning community requires commitment to all three kinds of knowledge.

Questions for Discussion

Build a list of examples of where you find each kind of knowledge in your church. Which of the three kinds of knowledge seems most prevalent? Which is lacking?

If improvement knowledge were emphasized in your church, what changes might occur?

Who "walks the cat walk" in your church?

_____

_____

_____

_____

_____

_____

Discovery
Naming Our Current Reality

In answering the previous questions for discussion you listed examples of each of the three kinds of knowledge found in your congregation's life. Each individual in your church has a varying degree of each kind of knowledge. For example, someone may have great knowledge of leadership while having little or no spiritual knowledge. Or, a person can be bursting with spiritual fervor but have no clue about improvement knowledge.

In our day, as people come to the church seeking spirituality for their lives, we are beginning to encounter more and more individuals with a mix of experience. It would be an error to believe that every adult is equipped with the same levels of knowledge in each of the areas. Still, how many of our churches have only one adult Christian education class as if all adults are at the same place in their journey?

We know that learning is a lifelong endeavor. We can always grow in professional knowledge. We believe we can also grow in our spiritual knowledge. What happens when improvement knowledge enters the mix is a marvelous journey of maturing faith. Imagine the Christian journey not as a linear experience (directional flow), but as a trip up a mountain around which the trail constantly ascends higher and higher as we travel along encircling the peak (spiral flow). Our primary task is the making of disciples in order to transform the world. Disciples are made as people move through the processes of our church and continue to grow in their faith and trust in God. At the same time we must be ready to improve those processes in order to respond to the needs of our people.

Every ministry process in the church employs all three types of knowledge. For example, there is a fundamental "knowledge" that Christian education is important for developing faithful disciples. Through prayer, conversation, meditation, and worship, people grow in their understanding of God. Spiritual knowledge undergirds authentic Christian education, but spiritual knowledge alone is not enough. Academic study of God, the Bible, Jesus Christ, and theology expands the knowledge base for Christian education. Professional knowledge is imperative for continuous growth and learning.

Improvement knowledge also promotes Christian education by enabling Christian disciples to see how their learning influences their daily lives. What we know about God influences how we think about ourselves, our neighbors, our coworkers, and our families. Our faith affects how we see our culture, how we relate to our communities, and how we choose our values.

It is helpful to be able to understand how these three types of knowledge exist and are interdependent in our faith quest.

Exercise

On newsprint, reproduce Figure 11A. Looking at each of the areas of ministry listed in the first column, move across the chart identifying what role spiritual knowledge, professional knowledge, and improvement knowledge play in that ministry. Keeping in mind that the three kinds of knowledge overlap, pay attention to their interrelatedness. Discuss how each kind of knowledge is vital for creating faith-forming communities. How would paying closer attention to improvement knowledge strengthen any of these ministries?

For Resources, Teaching Aids, and Newest Information

Check out our website at www.faithquest.net.

Figure 11A

AREA OF MINISTRY	SPIRITUAL KNOWLEDGE	PROFESSIONAL KNOWLEDGE	IMPROVEMENT KNOWLEDGE
Worship\Prayer			
Study of Scripture\ Christian Conferencing			
Community\Fellowship Building			
Acts of Mercy\Service			

SESSION 12:
Becoming the Body of Christ

Scriptures:
- Ephesians 3:1–4:24
  Focus Verses: Ephesians 4:7-16

Key Biblical Concepts:
- The body of Christ
- Spiritual gifts
- Christian vocation

Key Concepts for the Journey:
- Spiritual gifts discovery
- Specialization
- Continuous improvement

Outline:
- Gathering
- A Time of Centering
- Prayer
- Preparation
  Questions and Answers
- Exploration
  A Reflective Moment Along the Way
  Questions and Small-Group Exercises
- Discovery
- Conclusion

Introduction

The apostle Paul offers a compelling vision for the church. Paul employs an organic, dynamic image of the human body as a metaphor for the church. Christ is the head, and each one of God's children assumes the place of one part of the body. Paul stresses the interdependence of the individual parts, and he makes a strong case for the need for Christian community. In 1 Corinthians 12, Romans 12, and Ephesians 4, Paul lists twenty different gifts of the Holy Spirit that God gives us to "knit us together" into the body of Christ. For Paul, the church is Christian men and women living out of the empowerment of their spiritual gifts and using those gifts in connection with Christ and with one another to be the incarnate body of Christ on earth.

The church of the early twenty-first century is reawakening to the gifts of the Holy Spirit. Popular theology of the eighteenth century, including that of John Wesley, taught that the time for spiritual gifts was past. Today, we are experiencing a renaissance of interest in these gifts. If the church is truly defined by God-given gifts, then the question emerges, "How can we faithfully serve God and neighbor without clarity about our gifts and how to use them?" Learning communities committed to quality ministry are seeking a deep and meaningful understanding of their spiritual gifts for ministry.

Prayer

God of all good gifts, we thank you for this time of exploration and growth. It is humbling to realize that we are gifted to be in your service and that you call us to live faithfully out of our gifts. Make us good stewards of the resources we control: our time, our energy, our minds, our gifts, our material resources, and our faith. Knit us together as an authentic Christian community, so that we may model to the world what it means to be the body of Christ. We ask this in Jesus' name. Amen.

FaithQuest: A New Way of Thinking About the World

Preparation
Daily Scripture References and Questions for Reflection

Day 1 — Ephesians 3:1-13
What is the "mystery of Christ" that Paul speaks of in this passage? What is the meaning of this mystery for today's church?

Day 2 — Ephesians 3:14-21
How does Paul's blessing and prayer provide a model for us in the present day? How does Paul's prayer define his understanding of the primary work of the church?

Day 3 — Ephesians 4:1-6
In what ways does your congregation model unity and oneness? How can a congregation move toward a deeper singleness of vision and purpose?

Day 4 — Ephesians 4:7-16
Why does God give us spiritual gifts? Why is it important that we clearly identify the gifts that God gives us?

Day 5 — Ephesians 4:17-24
What does it mean to "put away your former way of life" and to "clothe yourselves with the new self"? (Compare this passage with Colossians 3:5-17.) How does the image of putting on clothing apply to living a Christian life?

Day 6
Read the session material in preparation for your group experience. Begin to reflect on the questions to be discussed by your group.

Exploration
Background Information: The Body of Christ

One of the most compelling images in the Pauline epistles is that of the body of Christ. Easily accessible to every audience, it has a universal frame of reference. Once an audience understood the metaphor, it became a visionary image for the creation of the Christian community. Christian literature throughout history has employed and built upon this one image. In every generation, the concept of the body of Christ has exerted significant influence.

In the early Christian communities, division arose over who should lead and who should follow. There were often great rifts within communities, and both men and women struggled for supremacy among the community leaders. Competition arose concerning which gifts and abilities were most necessary for leadership. Paul's use of the body imagery allowed him to challenge the tensions in a non-confrontational way. Paul made it clear that each part of the body was necessary for the health of the whole. He shifted the focus from individual parts to the system—the working of the whole. It makes no difference that a finger might favor itself as superior to a toe. Stub that toe, and the entire body must respond. Lose that toe, and the body suffers loss of balance. Break that toe, and the body is less able to move quickly, potentially lessening the work that the finger can accomplish.

Interdependency was not simply a good idea at the time the epistle to the Ephesians was composed. It was imperative for the emerging Christian communities to develop strong identities in the face of rising persecution. Early Christianity tore families and existing communities apart. It touched deep emotions concerning heritage, religious identity, and tradition. Christianity caused a great deal of anger, and violence resulted. Christians were tormented by the Jews for not being Jewish and by the Romans for being Jewish. Christian communities needed to be united to face such persecution.

Throughout the letter to the Ephesians, the author brings a message of unity, proclaiming that the dividing walls of anger, pride, and hostility have been broken by the grace and love of Christ. Knit together as one body under Christ, the community has all it needs to stand fast in the face of danger and potential destruction.

To be strong, each member of the community must contribute to the greater good. The Pauline writer explains that by using God-given spiritual gifts, the community will gain its identity, strength, and place in the world.

Spiritual Gifts

Jesus never spoke of spiritual gifts, although he frequently referred to the empowerment of the Holy Spirit. Jesus embodied the gifts of the Spirit, and many of these gifts were manifest in the disciples. However, spiritual gifts were not identified and named until Paul's letters did so. See the references in Figure 12A.

When we speak of spiritual gifts in the New Testament, we use the terminology that Paul employed as he took the gospel message to the Gentile world. In Greek and Roman mythology, gods frequently bestowed powers upon human beings who found favor with them. Wisdom, knowledge, healing, discernment, prophecy, teaching, and leadership were highly prized attributes in the Greek-speaking culture. Worshipers appealed to their gods for these "gifts."

In the Greek and Roman cultures, the receipt of a spiritual gift was a sign of blessing. Those so blessed claimed privileged positions within their community. Such privilege gave rise to divisiveness, which is addressed in all three of the Pauline epistles that deal with spiritual gifts. Paul transformed the understanding of spiritual giftedness from something that set people apart to something that brought them together.

The emerging Christian church was open to teachings about spiritual giftedness. The issue of spiritual giftedness is a fine example of adapting the gospel message to communicate to a different culture—without compromising the integrity of the message. Paul defined the church for a foreign audience in a way that provided a deep understanding of God. By Paul's definition, the church is where God provides all the necessary gifts and resources through individuals who join together to become one single body under the lordship of Jesus the Christ. The church is not a location—a place where people gather; the church exists wherever gifted men and women travel upon the earth. This definition is no less valid today than it was twenty centuries ago. In fact, this definition is fully harmonious with the vision that Jesus offered of the kingdom of God. The kingdom of God is that place where God provides all the necessary gifts and resources to the people who form the body of Christ.

A significant result of this definition of the church is that every member has a role to play. No one is passive. Each person is gifted and is expected to employ that gift for the common good.

Christianity emerged with Christ at the head. Although people were set apart to lead the church, they were still part of the *laos*, the whole people of God working together. Pastors (shepherds), prophets, and leaders are measured equally with helpers, servants, the compassionate, and administrators. No human being had the right to lord over any other. The community set standards and rules—a radical paradigm shift for both Jew and Gentile.

Christian Vocation

Through the centuries, the idea of a "call" into ministry has undergone many changes. At various times, "call" has been reserved for the chosen few—those set apart from the rest of the church to provide word, order, and sacrament to communities and congregations. At other times, "call" has been interpreted broadly to mean an open summons to anyone who calls herself or himself Christian. Today, "call" is most readily defined as a direct "summons" from God to enter into the professional ministry. Many lay ministers feel invalidated by this limited definition. What causes the real dilemma is the confusion between the terms "call" and "vocation." Simply stated, a specialized call may be a unique and rare occurrence, but Christian vocation is available to all. We all have been gifted by God, and God intends for us to engage in specialized work.

The early Christian church transformed the concept of church leadership. Women figured prominently in the first-century church (though they were quickly denied this power as the church became institutionalized); tradespeople and common workers shared in leadership. Property was shared among the members of the community, effectively erasing class distinctions. The question was not, "Am I called to ministry?" but "In what way have I been called to ministry?" Christian communities took seriously the need to explore ways to use spiritual gifts and to make certain that everyone participated in the "building of the body."

Vocation, a call to serve, is God's summons to all Christians. To acknowledge that God has gifted us to perform specific ministries engages us in both discipleship and stewardship. We move beyond asking what the church has to offer us to discerning what we have to offer the world as Christ's body. We do not exist simply to form a community; rather, the community forms to fulfill the summons of God. We are brought together to engage in the work of Kingdom-building. Christian vocation reminds us that we are to be doers of the word, not merely hearers.

A Reflective Moment Along the Way

In the metaphor of the body of Christ, every part of the body is vital to the health of the living body of Christ in the world today. Think about this image of the church, especially regarding your congregation.

How healthy is our body today? Is our body whole? If not, what parts (which people) are missing? What keeps us from being fully in union with Christ?

Be prepared to talk about your reflections with the FaithQuest group. Pause to offer a prayer before you continue.

Key Concepts for the Journey
Spiritual Gifts Discovery

Take a moment to compare the three lists (in Figure 12A) of spiritual gifts that appear in the Pauline epistles. What similarities do you notice? What differences?

The Pauline letters describe twenty different spiritual gifts. Each list is fundamentally different from the others. In the same way that no individual (with perhaps the exception of Jesus Christ) possesses all the gifts, no congregation possesses all the gifts. For too long, churches have felt compelled to offer every possible ministry. As a result, some ministries have been of poor quality, and church members have been asked to perform tasks that they were ill-equipped to handle.

The church as activity center sets itself up for mediocrity. People have settled for first and second levels of quality (assumed, desired), while sacrificing the third level of quality (unexpected) that could delight and transform the people we serve. (See Session 7 for a review of the three levels of quality.) From Paul's letters, it appears that God's intention is that we do what we are gifted to do and that we leave the things for which we are not gifted to the individuals and communities that are better suited for them. In a connectional system, this concept shouldn't be difficult to understand. Connectional churches should view themselves as gifted members of a larger body. What one congregation is unable to do can be accomplished by a nearby sister congregation.

There is no particular order of importance to the spiritual gifts in the lists. Spiritual gifts are relatively equal in importance. It is the combination—the way they are used in relationship to one another—that truly makes the difference. In fact, Paul spends the most time describing the spiritual gifts in 1 Corinthians, but then says that love is greater than any or all of the gifts combined.

The spiritual gifts are tools given by God to ensure that the work begun in Jesus Christ would continue in the world. Spiritual gifts are Kingdom-building tools. Like any tools, they are useful only if the person using them is skilled. Further, as with any tool, spiritual gifts benefit no one unless they are used. A critical question for today's church is "How well do we enable people to use their God-given gifts?"

Many congregations struggle with how to answer this question. The vast majority of them need to ask first, "What gifts do we possess?" and "What should we be doing with them?" Most congregations need a process for discovering, developing, and deploying their spiritual gifts.

Dozens of tools are available to help people discover their spiritual gifts. They are not scientific or infallible, but they do provide a context for beginning the discovery process. One spiritual-gifts discovery tool is about as good as any other, with just a couple of exceptions. Some gifts-discovery tools use a questionable methodology of looking at what we have in today's church, then "proof-texting" Scripture to find support. Some tools include things like music and humor as spiritual gifts. While these are important elements for community building, there is no real support for them as spiritual gifts.

Any spiritual-gifts discovery tool is simply a means to an end. The Bible is fully adequate to get the discussion and exploration under way. Paul had no "tools" for discovering spiritual gifts; he simply employed discernment, and each community developed its gifts together. Spiritual-gifts discovery is a critical work of Christian community. It is not an individual process but a communal sharing where people help one another identify gifts and graces.

Identification of gifts is the starting place. The next step is to develop the gifts. We need to develop

Figure 12A

ROMANS 12:6-8	1 CORINTHIANS 12:8-10, 28-30	EPHESIANS 4:11-12
prophecy serving teaching exhortation giving leadership compassion	wisdom knowledge faith healing working of miracles prophecy discernment various tongues interpretation of tongues apostleship teaching helping administration	apostleship prophecy evangelism shepherding teaching

professional spiritual-gifts knowledge: What is our gift all about? What does it do? How have others used it? What must we do to use this gift well? These questions require study, conversation, trial and error, practice, and prayer. Once this work of spiritual-gifts development occurs, there is still more to do.

If we do not have adequate outlets for our spiritual gifts, then we are guilty of poor stewardship. An underused (or unused) gift is a wasted gift. Congregations need to find ways to help members use their spiritual gifts. They need to know how spiritual gifts blend together to create settings for effective ministry and service. Congregations need to be able to apply improvement knowledge to the process of spiritual-gifts discovery.

The work of spiritual-gifts discovery, development, and deployment is an ongoing process in the life of a Christian community. There is reawakened interest in spiritual gifts, and many congregations are redesigning to be gifts-based ministry systems.

One important thing to remember is that spiritual gifts are not given so that we might support the work of the church in the activity-center paradigm. We do not help people find their gifts so that they might support the work of the institution. We help people find their gifts so that they can live as faithful disciples in the world and so that the community of faith can build itself around the God-given gifts for effective service.

Specialization

We live in an age of specialization. Organizations focus attention on a niche where they can provide quality products or services. Professionals provide specialized services in one or two areas. The current thinking is that it is better to excel in one area than to be average in many. This message is often lost on today's mainline churches.

Surprisingly, specialization in the Christian community is not a new idea. In fact, it is evident throughout the New Testament. Jesus gave the disciples very simple instructions: teach, preach, heal. Paul identified churches by the work for which they were known. Even the seven letters to the churches in the Book of Revelation identify each church by specific qualities, both good and bad. It was understood that individual communities possessed certain strengths, and it was assumed that each built upon those strengths.

The concept of specialization in the New Testament also extends to individuals. In 1 Corinthians 3, Paul addresses divisions in the church at Corinth and the concern about whether the church should follow him or Apollos. Paul says that Apollos is no better or worse than he is. Paul understood that he and Apollos possessed different gifts, and that both were necessary. Paul says, "I planted, Apollos watered, but God gave the growth" (1 Corinthians 3:6). Their gifts in combination allowed good things to happen. The implication is clear: Paul could not do what Apollos did; Apollos could not do what Paul did; but both men were vitally important.

The concept of specialization is a freeing idea for the church. It takes the pressure off individual congregations—especially smaller churches—to do everything well. If a congregation is gifted in the areas of knowledge, wisdom, teaching, shepherding, and discernment, but is weak in apostleship, evangelism, compassion, and serving, then it should help people live out of their gifts and put all its energy into being a quality teaching church, instead of worrying about outreach programs. An effective teaching church draws as many new believers as evangelizing churches whose members go out and knock on doors. If a church is deeply gifted with evangelists, prophets, leaders, and apostles, it should be free to move into the community in a variety of ways without feeling guilty that it does not provide the liveliest worship or educational opportunities. Who says that every church must do everything well? Where is it written that a church must offer a traditional Sunday school program? A few churches realize that they do not have gifts for education, so they focus their energies elsewhere. Which honors God best: offering a high-quality ministry in a single area of service, or offering a smorgasbord of fair- to low-quality ministries that burden church members and dissipate their energy and interest? We dishonor God when we squander our gifts, and we dishonor one another when we invite people to serve outside the bounds of their basic gifts. As the church, we should offer people opportunities to serve where they will thrive and be successful Christian stewards.

Specialization is not a way to protect ourselves from doing ministries we don't like. It is a way for us to focus on the gifts that we have been given, to live powerfully from our gifts in our day-to-day lives, and to design ministry systems in our faith-forming communities that fully use those gifts—and to forego other areas of ministry for which we are less gifted—without feeling guilty.

Specialization will encourage us to become the church we say we are. If we focus on our strengths, then we will also need to be aware of our weaknesses; and we will need to be aware of the churches in our connection that compensate for our weaknesses. We need to have the courage and integrity to say to newcomers, "We may not have what you are looking for here, but we do know of a church nearby that is gifted in that area." This is true connectionalism.

Continuous Improvement

The screen saver on a young pastor's computer repeats the word "better" over and over. She says this is her reminder that no matter how good she has gotten at any aspect of her ministry, she still has room to improve. Such an attitude is at the heart of quality, and it is the definition of continuous improvement. Being better is a process with no end. We never truly arrive at the destination of "better." In the areas of spiritual giftedness and specialization, a commitment to "better" is crucial.

Even in our existing structures and systems for ministry, a commitment to continuous improvement would be a blessing. Much of what we do is oriented toward a short-term goal that allows us to give less than our best. Our standards have slipped, and we can't understand why we struggle. One church allowed Sunday school students to miss seven classes out of thirty-six and still receive a "perfect attendance" pin at the end of the year. Local churches and annual conferences fund their budgets at seventy-five to eighty percent and report that they "exceeded their expectations" for the year. When we lower our standards, we pay a price. When we set the floor as our target, we guarantee we will hit it. All we have to do is fall over. But if we choose to set our sights higher, then we need to develop systems that will enable us to improve. Our current systems do not provide us that support. New systems for a new millennium, based on people-focused, Spirit-empowered, continuously improving processes are the key.

Questions for Discussion

What are the prominent gifts of the people who come to your church? How do you help people discover and develop their gifts? How do you help people live out of their gifts in their daily lives?

For what ministries is your church known? How have you specialized based on the strengths of your gifts as a congregation? What can you do to use your gifts better in the ministries you perform?

What processes do you use to improve your ministries? In what ways do you encourage and assist individuals within your congregation to improve?

_____

_____

_____

_____

_____

_____

Discovery
Naming Our Current Reality

Spiritual-gifts discovery begins with an understanding of the spiritual gifts. Below are some brief definitions of the twenty gifts listed in Scripture[13]:

Administration — The gift of organizing human and material resources for the work of Christ, including the ability to plan and work with people to delegate responsibilities, track progress, and evaluate the effectiveness of procedures. Administrators attend to details, communicate effectively, and take as much pleasure in working behind the scenes as they do in standing in the spotlight.

Apostleship — The gift of spreading the gospel of Jesus Christ to other cultures and foreign lands. This is the missionary zeal that moves us from the familiar into uncharted territory to share the good news. Apostles embrace opportunities to learn foreign languages, visit other cultures, and go to places where people have not had the opportunity to hear the Christian message. The United States of America is fast becoming a mission field of many languages and cultures. It is no longer necessary to cross an ocean to enter the mission field. Even across generations, we may find that we need to "speak other languages" just to communicate.

Compassion — This gift is exceptional empathy with those in need that moves us to action. More than just concern, compassion demands that we share the suffering of others in order to connect the gospel truth with other realities of life. Compassion moves us beyond our comfort zones to offer practical, tangible aid to all God's children, regardless of the worthiness of the recipients or the response we receive for our service.

Discernment — This is the ability to separate truth from erroneous teachings and to rely on spiritual intuition to know what God is calling us to do. Discernment allows us to focus on what is truly important and to ignore that which deflects us from faithful obedience to God. Discernment aids us in knowing whom to listen to and whom to avoid.

Evangelism — This is the ability to share the gospel of Jesus Christ with those who have not heard it before or with those who have not yet made a decision for Christ. This gift is manifested in both one-on-one situations and in group settings, large and small. It is an intimate relationship with another person or persons that requires the sharing of personal faith experience and a call for a response of faith to God.

Exhortation — This is the gift of exceptional encouragement. Exhorters see the silver lining in every cloud, offer deep and inspiring hope to the fellowship, and look for and commend the best in everyone. Exhorters empower the community of faith to feel good about itself and to feel hopeful for the future. Exhorters are not concerned by appearances; they hold fast to what they know to be true and right and good.

Faith — More than just belief, faith is a gift that empowers an individual or a group to hold fast to identity in Christ in the face of any challenge. The gift of faith enables believers to rise above pressures and problems that might otherwise cripple them. Faith is characterized by an unshakable trust in God to deliver on God's promises, no matter what. The gift of faith inspires those who might be tempted to give up to hold on.

Giving — Beyond the regular response of gratitude to God that all believers make, giving as a gift is the ability to use the resource of money to support the work of the body of Christ. Giving is the ability to manage money to the honor and glory of God. Givers can discern the best ways to put money to work, can understand the validity and practicality of appeals for funds, and can guide church leaders in the most faithful methods for managing the congregation's finances.

Healing — This is the gift of channeling God's healing powers into the lives of God's people. Physical, emotional, spiritual, and psychological healing are all ways that healers manifest this gift. Healers are prayerful, and they help people understand that healing is in the hands of God and that healing is often more than just erasing negative symptoms. Some of the most powerful healers display some of the most heartbreaking afflictions.

Helping — This is the gift of making sure that everything is ready for the work of Christ to occur. Helpers assist others to accomplish the mission and ministry of the church. These "unsung heroes" work behind the scenes and attend to details that others would rather not be bothered with. Helpers function faithfully, regardless of the credit or attention they receive. Helpers provide the framework upon which the ministry of the church is built.

Interpretation of Tongues (*see also* Tongues) — This gift has two very different meanings: (1) The ability to interpret *foreign* languages without the necessity of formal study to communicate with those who have not heard the Christian message; or (2) the ability to interpret the gift of tongues as a *secret prayer language* that communicates with God at a deep spiritual level. Both understandings are communal in nature: the first extends the good news into the world; the second strengthens the faith within the fellowship.

Knowledge — This is the gift of knowing the truth through faithful study of the Scripture and the human situation. Knowledge provides the information necessary for the transformation of the world and formation of the body of Christ. Those possessing this gift challenge the fellowship to improve itself through study, reading of Scripture, discussions, and prayer.

Leadership — This is the gift of orchestrating the gifts and resources of others to achieve the mission and ministry of the church. Leaders move the community of faith toward a God-given vision of service, and they enable others to use their gifts to the very best of their abilities. Leaders are capable of creating synergy, whereby the community of faith accomplishes much more than its individual members could achieve on their own.

Miracle Working — This gift enables the church to operate at a spiritual level that recognizes the miraculous work of God in the world. Miracle workers invoke God's power to accomplish that which appears impossible by worldly standards. Miracle workers remind the fellowship of the extraordinary nature of the ordinary world, thereby increasing faithfulness and trust in God. Miracle workers pray for God to work in the lives of others, and they feel no sense of surprise when their prayers are answered.

Prophecy — This is the gift of speaking the Word of God clearly and faithfully. Prophets allow God to speak through them to communicate the message that people most need to hear. While often unpopular, prophets are able to say what needs to be said because of the spiritual empowerment they receive. Prophets do not foretell the future but proclaim God's future by revealing God's perspective on our current reality.

Servanthood — This is the gift of serving the spiritual and material needs of other people within and beyond the local church. Servants understand their place in the body of Christ as giving comfort and aid to all who are in need. Servants look to the needs of others rather than focusing on their own needs. To serve is to put faith into action; it is to treat others as if they were indeed Jesus Christ himself. The gift of service extends our Christian love into the world.

Shepherding — This is the gift of guidance. Shepherds nurture other Christians in the faith and provide a mentoring relationship to those who are new to the faith. Displaying an unusual spiritual maturity, shepherds share from their experience and learning to facilitate the spiritual growth and development of others. Shepherds take individuals under their care and walk with them on their spiritual journeys. Many shepherds provide spiritual direction and guidance to a wide variety of believers.

Teaching — This is the gift of bringing scriptural and spiritual truths to others. More than just teaching church school, teachers witness to the truth of Jesus Christ in a variety of ways, and they help others to understand the complex realities of the Christian faith. Teachers are revealers. They shine the light of understanding into the darkness of doubt and ignorance. They open people to new truths, and they challenge people to be more in the future than they have been in the past.

Tongues (*see also* Interpretation of Tongues) — This gift has two popular interpretations: (1) the ability to communicate the gospel to other people in a *foreign language* without the benefit of having studied said language (see Acts 2:4); or (2) the ability to speak to God in a secret, unknown *prayer language* that can only be understood by a person possessing the gift of interpretation. The gift of speaking in the language of another culture makes the gift of tongues valuable for spreading the gospel throughout the world, while the gift of speaking a secret prayer language offers the opportunity to build faithfulness within a community of faith.

Wisdom — This is the gift of translating life experience into spiritual truth and of seeing the application of scriptural truth to daily living. The wise Christians in our fellowships offer balance and understanding that transcend reason. Wisdom applies a God-given common sense to our understanding of God's plan for the church. Wisdom helps the community of faith remain focused on the important work of the church, and it enables newer, less mature Christians to benefit from those who have been blessed by God to share deep truths.

As we reflect on these gifts and on what they mean for our lives, we need to remember that although spiritual gifts define our place in the body of Christ, we are spiritually-gifted people seven days a week, in whatever arena of life we find ourselves. We must see how we can live out of our gifts as the church in every life setting. What does it mean to be a teacher at home, at work, at school, in public places? How do we shepherd outside the church? How do we use gifts such as discernment, faith, knowledge, and so on—in the secular sphere? The critical work of spiritual-gifts discovery is not to see how people fit into our system of the church, but to design a system of the church around the spiritual gifts that empower people to *be* the church everywhere in the world.

FaithQuest: A New Way of Thinking About the World

Exercise

Twenty spiritual gifts appear on the wheel of Figure 12B. There are three levels within the wheel: individual, church, and world. Take a moment to identify what you believe your gifts might be.[14] Then list ways in which you use or might use these gifts in the three different levels. Ask yourself: How do I use my gifts myself? How do I use them in my community of faith? How do I use them in and for the world?

What kinds of changes would you experience if you redesigned your church's ministry systems according to the spiritual giftedness of your leaders and congregation?

How will designing gifts-based ministries help you move from the activity-center paradigm into the faith-forming-community paradigm?

For Resources, Teaching Aids, and Newest Information

Check out our website at: www.faithquest.net.

CIRCLE OF GIFTS

Gifts on the wheel: Helping, Wisdom, Serving, Tongues, Administration, Discernment, Shepherding, Teaching, Knowledge, Interpretation of Tongues, Evangelism, Apostleship, Compassion, Exhortation, Leadership, Miracle, Giving, Faith, Prophecy, Healing.

Three levels: World, Church, Individual.

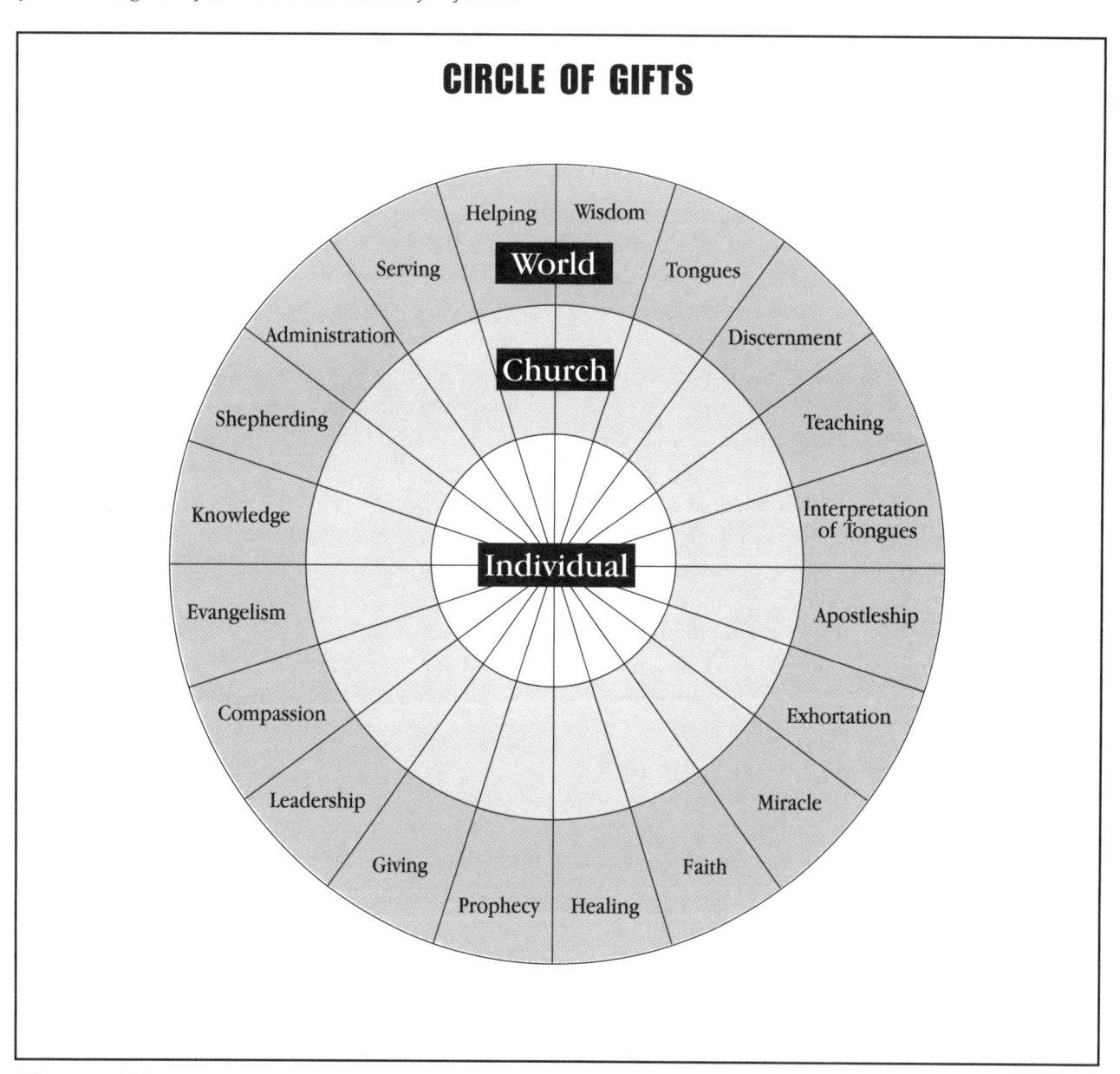

Figure 12B

SESSION 13:
New Rules for a New Reality

Scriptures:
- Ephesians 5:3–6:17
    Focus Verses: Ephesians 5:15-20

Key Biblical Concepts:
- *Haustafel*—House Rules
- Christian community in Ephesus

Key Concepts for the Journey:
- Defining current reality
- Learning new rules

Outline:
- Gathering
- A Time of Centering
- Prayer
- Preparation
    Questions and Answers
- Exploration
    A Reflective Moment Along the Way
    Questions and Small-Group Exercises
- Discovery
- Conclusion

Introduction

As society changes, so change the rules of conscience, comportment, and community. The letter to the Ephesians was written to help make the transition to a new way of living easier for first- and second-century Christians. This Pauline letter is all about change, and it offers new rules that define the new reality.

The Christian church at the threshold of the twenty-first century is a church in a changing world. With each new social change, the rules for living change. A church that is not involved in discovering, defining, and interpreting the new rules will have little influence on people's lives. A church that offers spiritual transformation and renewal is a church that knows the rules.

Prayer

Gracious and ever faithful God, we ask your help as we move through a fast-paced and constantly changing world. What we knew before is not always what we need to know today. Solutions to yesterday's problems no longer have meaning. Our understanding of reality shifts with each new scientific discovery. It is good to know that as the world races on, you stay with us, steadfast, reliable, and secure. You alone can comprehend the vastness of change in this world. Enable us to stand firm in our faith, while being flexible in our Christian service, that we might honor and glorify you in all our thoughts, words, and actions. We pray in Jesus' name. Amen.

Preparation
Daily Scripture References and Questions for Reflection

Day 1 — Ephesians 5:3-14
The Pauline author instructs us to "find out what is pleasing to the Lord." How do we do this? Individually? Corporately? Does "what is pleasing to the Lord" change from generation to generation?

_____

_____

_____

Day 2 — Ephesians 5:15-20

What is the meaning of the phrase "the days are evil"? What does this phrase mean for us today? In what ways is your congregation "making the most of the time"?

Day 3 — Ephesians 5:21-33

It is important to look beyond the patriarchal context in which the Pauline author writes to see the new ideas that he is offering. How does the writer challenge Christians in Ephesus to embrace a new model for marriage and family relationships?

Day 4 — Ephesians 6:1-9

How does the gospel of Jesus Christ establish new rules of conduct and relationship in these passages?

Day 5 — Ephesians 6:10-17

How do you understand the Pauline categories of our enemies: rulers, authorities, cosmic powers, and spiritual forces of evil? Looking beyond the military imagery, what is the author communicating to the church in Ephesus?

Day 6

Read the session material in preparation for your group experience.

Exploration
Background Information: "Haustafel"—House Rules

The letter to the Ephesians calls Christian believers to unity, to community, and to communion. It encourages them to adopt a new life, then it launches into a set of rules to define that new life. These rules are so specific as to redefine family and household conduct. German scholars have labeled these instructions *Haustafel*, literally "house table" or "rules."

It is important to understand what these new rules meant to the early Christian settlements. They challenged fundamental relationships and replaced age-old traditions. From the perspective of the twenty-first century, these are primitive and even uncivilized rules—very hierarchical and somewhat oppressive. Taken within the historical context, however, they are startlingly progressive and radical.

In primitive Palestine, women were afforded virtually no rights and privileges apart from family—first relating to the father, then to the husband. Widows were outcasts, with absolutely no support or aid. They were often victims of violence and abuse, and they often died of exposure and malnutrition shortly after being widowed. Wives were allowed few rights, and it was a sin for a woman to be present at the reading of the Torah. Religious instruction was restricted to men, and whatever religious instruction women received came through their husbands and families. Unmarried women were treated as property, and they held little or no value once they reached their late teens. Marriage contracts were made early, and they involved the exchange of property or livestock. Women were managers of the household affairs, producers of children, and caretakers of the needs of the men.

It is difficult for us to comprehend the revolutionary nature of the comparison of marriage to the relationship of Christ to the church. This simple analogy would have profound implications for all who heard it. It effectively redefined the entire marriage relationship within the confines of the dominant culture. Certainly, it was a far cry from fair and equitable, but it was light years ahead of the traditional understanding of marriage.

The same applies to the areas of children and slaves. While we understand slavery to be barbaric and evil, it was an accepted reality in the first century. The instructions to slave holders challenged the existent reality and provided a new basis for slave-master relationships in the early Christian communities. These new teachings had monumental impact, and they signaled to the rest of the world that the paradigm had shifted.

Christian Community in Ephesus

Ephesus was a crossroad of cultures, a cosmopolitan city, a center of trade, and a political gathering place. Known for its religiosity, Ephesus was home to the temple of Artemis. The city accommodated the worship of a wide variety of gods and goddesses. Because of the variety, divisions constantly arose; and the development of peaceful, lasting communities was difficult. The plea for unity that pervades Ephesians is reiterated in later writings of Ignatius and Clement. Unity, harmony, peace, cooperation: these were the critical issues for the Christian community in Ephesus.

Not only was there danger of internal division, but the church in Ephesus also faced many external pressures. Disharmony within, persecution without—all set within a multicultural social sphere—made the establishment of the church difficult. Our contemporary North American church bears a strong resemblance to the church in Ephesus at the end of the first century.

A Reflective Moment Along the Way

The events of September 11, 2001, changed the way many people view the world. New rules were called for to protect our people from the threat of terrorism. Americans are even willing to give up certain privacy freedoms in order to envision a safer society.

List some of the "new rules" Jesus initiated as part of his vision of the kingdom of God. After compiling the list, begin a second list. This time name "new rules" that you have come to value for your life as you have grown along your faith journey. Talk about your answers as you meet together. What new insights do you have?

Key Concepts for the Journey
Defining Current Reality

To define current reality as simply "what is" isn't accurate. Reality is subjective, not objective. Prior to Columbus, the world *was* flat. Prior to Copernicus, the earth *was* the center of the universe. Human beings couldn't fly . . . until they could! Reality changes, and what is "real" at one time may not be "real" at another time.

Reality relies as much on perception as on fact. The way an individual or group perceives reality defines the way the individual or group thinks and acts. Most prejudices have absolutely no bearing in actuality, but people behave as if their prejudices were true. We must understand the power of perception if we want to be effective in the work of transforming lives.

Who stands in the best position to define current reality? How do we gain perspective to be able to clearly define where we are? To whom do we listen?

Traditionally, the leaders of a local congregation defined their current reality by talking to one another about what the church was doing, how many people were showing up, how much money was in the plate each week, and how many children were in the Sunday school. If the numbers were up, then current reality was perceived to be very good. If the numbers were low, then the leaders called for change. Are these factors the best indicators of the current reality of a local church? Probably not. Although they provide some important data, they are limited.

The perspective of most people in leadership positions is that their church is doing pretty well—that it is friendly; that it provides meaningful worship, education, and fellowship experiences; and that it serves an important purpose in the community. Indeed, this is *their reality*. They probably wouldn't work so hard to support the church if they didn't feel this way. But is this the reality of the average pew-sitter on a Sunday morning? Of a visitor? Of an inactive member? Of a community member from another denomination?

Have you ever encountered a leader from another church who didn't list as one of his or her church's greatest attributes "We are a friendly church"?

Who decides whether a church is friendly or not? It doesn't matter if the entire leadership core of a local church perceives the church as friendly if that perception is not shared by visitors and infrequent attendees of the fellowship. Defining current reality requires the inclusion of a variety of perspectives.

In addition to focusing on the internal realities of the local congregation, we need to consider the current reality of the community in which the church is located and the current reality of the larger cultural context.

Each community is dealing with issues of politics, economics, education, crime, safety, healthcare, family, and myriad other concerns. Certain issues can hold an entire community in their grip. What is pressing and important one week may give way to something completely different a few short weeks later. It is important to determine the current reality of the local community to understand how the church can serve. Churches that serve their communities find that they are supported by members and nonmembers alike.

Beyond the local community, each church is influenced by the prevailing culture. Art, music, and literature have always shaped—and have been shaped by—the attitudes of people. Television exerts a powerful force on people's opinions and their understanding of the world. Computer technology and the Internet are reshaping the flow of information. We are fast becoming a global community. Politics, environmental issues, biotechnology, economics, and criminal justice are issues that sweep into our homes every day. These are just a few of the influences that define our current reality.

The church is in a unique position to help people make sense of their individual current realities, but the church will be ineffective until it can clearly and accurately define its own current reality. The church exists in a constantly changing world. People are seeking stable values and principles for living that can help them cope. They come into the church seeking a relationship with Jesus Christ. Most want nothing more than that, because they believe that a relationship with Christ can strengthen them to live their lives. Unless the leaders of a local church understand the many different realities in which people live today, they will miss many opportunities for service and disciple-making. The key is not to wait poised with a message to share, but to listen. Listening to the life stories of the men and women who enter our churches is the best way to define current reality.

In addition to listening, church leaders need to observe the world around them. They should spend an evening surfing television channels or the Internet, wander through a bookstore or a mall, take in a movie or two, scan the radio stations, browse through magazines and newspapers. Church leaders should pay attention to the global nature of news and business. The church of the twenty-first century will have a ministry that stretches around the planet.

What we identify as our current reality today will change. We cannot "lock in" a set of self-perpetuating programs or ministries. What people may need from us next year or what God may call us to do may be significantly different from what we are doing now. Flexibility is essential.

Learning New Rules

At a recent seminar, an older pastor left the room muttering, "I've been doing this for years. If I don't know how it's done yet, I need to retire." This attitude, while common, reflects a mode of thinking that is not helpful in the church. While experience is important, it is more important to be willing and able to change to meet the demands of new realities.

A group of United Methodist pastors was asked to list the top five news stories of the previous day. The group consisted of about sixty individuals, evenly divided between men and women, over forty and under forty. Of the pastors over forty years of age, almost ninety percent of them listed news stories about the United States. Of the pastors under forty, about fifty percent of them listed stories concerning the U.S. The younger pastors said that they regularly mentioned global issues in their sermons. The older clergy reported that they rarely, if ever, used global stories. The younger pastors said they took sermon illustrations from the Internet, from cable television, from *USA Today*, and from National Public Radio. The older pastors reported taking illustrations from *Reader's Digest*, local newspapers (including the comic strips), and from network television. The older pastors talked about the need to get out into the community to visit people and about the frustration of not finding people at home. The younger pastors talked about the ease with which they could communicate with parishioners by e-mail, phone, and fax.

It was interesting to note the contrast between the two groups (although there were some over-forties who fit more easily with the under-forties, and vice versa) and how troubling it was to the older clergy that the rules for ministry had changed. Instead of trying to figure out the new rules, they fought to play by the old rules. Each year, the rules change a bit more. The pastors who are willing to adapt will offer the most meaningful ministry.

The model of the learning community is critical for the health and well-being of the church. The ability to learn the new rules of an ever-shifting current reality will keep us on course toward the fulfillment of our vision for ministry. Without a system designed for learning and continuous improvement, we will be unable to reach out into a world that desperately needs the gospel message.

Throughout history, God has equipped the church for effective ministry. As Christianity spread around the globe, it met people where they were. Christianity has accommodated a wide variety of ideas, attitudes, and opinions without compromising the integrity of the gospel.

The United Methodist Church of the twenty-first century cannot afford to play by "church rules" of the 1950's, 60's, and 70's. Learning communities learn new rules quickly and create a relevant and inspiring vision for the future.

Questions for Discussion

In what ways does the perception of current reality differ between the active and inactive members of the congregation? How is your church perceived within the community?

How have the "rules" changed for the church in the past ten to twenty years? In what ways have you been flexible? In what ways have you held rigidly to the rules of the past?

Speculate on what the new rules will be in the faith-forming-community paradigm. What rules from the activity-center paradigm will need to be broken to enable us to create these new rules?

_____

_____

_____

_____

_____

Discovery
Naming Our Current Reality

Naming our current reality is a complex and demanding task. Because current reality is affected by many different perspectives, it is important to view reality from a variety of points of view.

Exercise

Demographers have long realized that different age groups, racial/ethnic groups, and sexes hold very different perspectives on many key issues. As you

FaithQuest: A New Way of Thinking About the World

These charts are samples you can use and modify for the discovery exercise described below. Reproduce the charts on large pieces of newsprint, leaving plenty of space to fill in information. Be sure to fill in first-hand reports from individuals in each category—do not fill in assumptions and stereotypes.

	MILLENNIAL GENERATION (1982–1999)	POSTMODERN GENERATION (1964–1981)	BABY BOOMERS (1946–1963)	PIONEER GENERATION (1928–1945)	G.I. GENERATION (1910–1927)	WOMEN	MEN
Work							
Family							
Play							
Faith							

Figure 13A

What are some of the rules that each of these groups operate by in these different settings? ("Rules" are standards of conduct, expectations, sense of purpose, benefits received, and so forth.)

	AFRICAN AMERICAN	HISPANIC	KOREAN	EUROPEAN AMERICAN	CARIBBEAN BLACK	1st-GENERATION IMMIGRANT
Work						
Family						
Play						
Faith						

Figure 13B

When you reproduce this chart, insert column headings that reflect the population of your church and your community. What are some of the rules that each of these racial/ethnic groups operate by in the different settings? Remember that "rules" are standards of conduct, expectations, benefits received, and so forth.

work to identify the current reality in your church, you will want to listen to a carefully segmented sample of people. Using the format above, gather the information requested and share the results in your group. See if there are other ways to apply this format within the church to gather other perspectives.

In each category, look for some of the "rules" unique to that group and look for similarities among the groups. See how other perspectives match and contrast with your own.

For Resources, Teaching Aids, and Newest Information

Check out our website at www.faithquest.net.

SECTION 4
The Teachings of John Wesley

A New Way of Thinking About the Christian Life

The United Methodist Church traces its roots to John Wesley, a priest in the Anglican Church. Wesley disagreed with many of the standards and practices of the Anglican Church, and his passion for bringing the gospel of Jesus Christ to the world moved him outside the confines of brick and mortar to the open air.

This section focuses on the teachings of John Wesley and the doctrine of The United Methodist Church while offering supportive Scriptural study for each day as well. Wesley's teachings help us understand what it means to be the church, and they open for us "A New Way of Thinking About the Christian Life."

SESSION 14:
The More Excellent Way

Key Wesleyan Concepts:
- Standards of Christian conduct
- Spiritual discipline
- The love of God

Key Concepts for the Journey:
- Discipleship, Stewardship, and Fellowship

Outline:
- Gathering
- A Time of Centering
- Prayer
- Preparation
    Questions and Answers
- Exploration
    A Reflective Moment Along the Way
    Questions and Small-Group Exercises
- Discovery
- Conclusion

Introduction

John Wesley believed that the world could be transformed into the kingdom of God. Through spreading "scriptural holiness across the land," Wesley felt that the church could bring about such transformation. This change would happen one person at a time; and by connecting new believers in Christian community, the influence of Jesus Christ would spread. This work of transformation defined the mission of the church for Wesley.

Wesley's sermon "The More Excellent Way" provides a look at his thinking and at his instructions for a church struggling to break free from malaise. The sermon also reveals Wesley's vision for growth and improvement.

Prayer

Gracious God, what we are today is not what you have called us to be. No matter how far we have come in our walk of faith, we still have room for growth. It is easy to be satisfied and to rest on our accomplishments, but such an attitude will do nothing to transform the world. There is no such thing as "good enough" when it comes to being your church. Grant us a spirit of continuous improvement, that we might do even more to honor and glorify the name of Jesus the Christ. Amen.

Preparation
Daily Reading and Questions for Reflection

Day 1 — excerpt from John Wesley's sermon "The More Excellent Way"[15]

In the preceding verses [to 1 Corinthians 12:31], St. Paul has been speaking of the extraordinary gifts of the Holy Ghost; such as healing the sick; prophesying, in the proper sense of the word, that is, foretelling things to come; speaking with strange tongues, such as the speaker had never learned; and the miraculous interpretation of tongues. And these gifts the Apostle allows to be desirable; yea, he exhorts the Corinthians, at least the teachers among them, (to whom chiefly, if not solely, they were wont to be given in the first ages of the Church,) to *covet* them *earnestly*, that thereby they might be qualified to be more useful either to Christians or Heathens. "And yet," says he, "I show unto you a more excellent way;" far more desirable than all these put together: Inasmuch as it will infallibly lead you to happiness, both in this world and in the world to come; whereas you might have all those gifts, yea, in the highest degree, and yet be miserable both in time and eternity....

However, I would not at present speak of these, of the extraordinary gifts of the Holy Ghost, but of the ordinary; and these likewise we may "covet earnestly," in order to be more useful in our generation. With this view, we may covet "the gift of *convincing speech,*" in order to "sound the unbelieving heart;" and the gift of *persuasion,* to move the affections, as well as enlighten the understanding. We may covet *knowledge,* both of the word and of the works of God, whether of providence or grace. We may desire a measure of that *faith* which, on particular occasions, wherein the glory of God or the happiness of men is nearly concerned, goes far beyond the power of natural causes. We may desire an easy elocution, a pleasing address, with resignation to the will of our Lord; yea, whatever would enable us, as we have opportunity, to be useful wherever we are. These gifts we may innocently desire; but there is "a more excellent way."

The way of love,—of loving all men for God's sake; of humble, gentle, patient love,—is that which the Apostle so admirably describes in the ensuing chapter. And without this, he assures us, all eloquence, all knowledge, all faith, all works, and all sufferings are of no more value in the sight of God than sounding brass or a rumbling cymbal, and are not of the least avail toward our eternal salvation. Without this, all we know, all we believe, all we do, all we suffer, will profit us nothing in the great day of accounts.

Question: What are the marks of the "more excellent way" that Wesley uses to define the practice of Christian believers?

Scripture Reflection: 1 Corinthians 12:27-31
The Corinthian church was apparently experiencing strife and disagreement. In what ways do this passage from Paul's letter and Wesley's words to the church of his day relate?

Day 2 — excerpt from John Wesley's sermon "The More Excellent Way"[16]

But at present I would take a different view of the text, and point out a "more excellent way" in another sense. It is the observation of an ancient writer, that there have been from the beginning two orders of Christians. The one lived an innocent life, conforming in all things, not sinful, to the customs and fashions of the world; doing many good works, abstaining from gross evils, and attending the ordinances of God. They endeavoured, in general, to have a conscience void of offence in their behaviour, but did not aim at any particular strictness, being in most things like their neighbours. The other Christians not only abstained from all appearance of evil, were zealous of good works in every kind, and attended all the ordinances of God, but likewise used all diligence to attain the whole mind that was in Christ, and laboured to walk, in every point, as their beloved Master. In order to this, they walked in a constant course of universal self-denial, trampling on every pleasure which they were not divinely conscious prepared them for taking pleasure in God. They took up their cross daily. They strove, they agonized without intermission, to enter in at the strait gate. This one thing they did, they spared no pains to arrive at the summit of Christian holiness; "leaving the first principles of the doctrine of Christ, to go on to perfection;" to "know all that love of God which passeth knowledge, and to be filled with all the fulness of God."

From long experience and observation I am inclined to think, that whoever finds redemption in the blood of Jesus, whoever is justified, has then the choice of walking in the higher or the lower path. I believe the Holy Spirit at that time sets before him the "more excellent way," and incites him to walk therein; to choose the narrowest path in the narrow way; to aspire after the heights and depths of holiness,—after the entire image of God. But if he does not accept this offer, he insensibly declines into the lower order of Christians. He still goes on in what may be called a good way, serving

God in his degree, and finds mercy in the close of life, through the blood of the covenant.

Question: What are the two orders of Christians? How does your church challenge you to choose this higher order of the "more excellent way"?

Scripture Reflection: Psalm 8
If we are made as human beings "a little lower than God," what implication does that suggest for our personal spiritual journey?

_____

_____

_____

_____

Day 3 — excerpt from John Wesley's sermon "The More Excellent Way"[17]

To begin at the beginning of the day. It is the manner of the generality of Christians, if they are not obliged to work for their living, to rise, particularly in winter, at eight or nine in the morning, after having lain in bed eight or nine, if not more, hours. I do not say now, (as I should have been very apt to do fifty years ago,) that all who indulge themselves in this manner are in the way to hell. But neither can I say, they are in the way to heaven, denying themselves, and taking up their cross daily. Sure I am, there is "a more excellent way" to promote health both of body and mind. . . . It is, therefore, undoubtedly, the most excellent way, in defiance of fashion and custom, to take just so much sleep as experience proves our nature to require; seeing this is indisputably most conducive both to bodily and spiritual health. And why should not you walk in this way? Because it is difficult? Nay, with men it is impossible. But all things are possible with God; and by his grace, all things will be possible to *you*. Only continue instant in prayer, and you will find this not only possible, but easy: Yea, and it will be far easier to rise early constantly, than to do it sometimes. But then you must begin at the right end; if you would rise early, you must sleep early. Impose it upon yourself, unless when something extraordinary occurs, to go to bed at a fixed hour. Then the difficulty of it will soon be over; but the advantage of it will remain for ever.

The generality of Christians, as soon as they rise, are accustomed to use some kind of *prayer*; . . . surely there is "a more excellent way" of ordering our private devotions. What if you were to follow the advice given by that great and good man, Mr. Law, on this subject? Consider both your outward and inward state, and vary your prayers accordingly. For instance: Suppose your outward state is prosperous; suppose you are in a state of health, ease, and plenty, having your lot cast among kind relations, good neighbours, and agreeable friends, that love you, and you them; then your outward state manifestly calls for praise and thanksgiving to God. On the other hand, if you are in a state of adversity; if God has laid trouble upon your loins; if you are in poverty, in want, in outward distress; if you are in imminent danger; if you are in pain and sickness; then you are clearly called to pour out your soul before God in such prayer as is suited to your circumstances. In like manner you may suit your devotions to your inward state, the present state of your mind. Is your soul in heaviness, either from a sense of sin, or through manifold temptations? Then let your prayer consist of such confessions, petitions, and supplications as are agreeable to your distressed situation of mind. On the contrary, is your soul in peace? Are you rejoicing in God? Are his consolations not small with you? Then say, with the Psalmist, "Thou art my God, and I will love thee: Thou art my God, and I will praise thee." You may, likewise, when you have time, add to your other devotions a little reading and meditation, and perhaps a psalm of praise,—the natural effusion of a thankful heart. You must certainly see, that this is "a more excellent way" than the poor dry form which you used before.

Question: Why are disciplines such as early rising, prayer, devotional reading, meditation, and so on important to faith formation and spiritual development?

Scripture Reflection: Psalm 18:6
Relationships of every kind need regular, open, and healthy communication. What does this verse (and others throughout the Psalm) tell us about ourselves? What about God? What about our relationship with God?

_____

_____

_____

_____

_____

Day 4 — excerpt from John Wesley's sermon "The More Excellent Way"[18]

The generality of Christians, after using some prayer, usually apply themselves to the *business* of their calling. Every man that has any pretence to be a Christian will not fail to do this; seeing it is impossible that an idle man can be a good man,—sloth being inconsistent with religion. But with what view, for what end, do you undertake and follow your worldly business? "To provide things necessary for myself and my family." It is a good answer, as far as it goes; but it does not go far enough. ...A Christian may go abundantly farther: His end in all his labour is, to please God; to do, not his own will, but the will of Him that sent him into the world,—for this very purpose, to do the will of God on earth as angels do in heaven. He works for eternity. He "labours not for the meat that perisheth," (this is the smallest part of his motive,) "but for that which endureth to everlasting life." And is not this "a more excellent way?"

Again: in what *manner* do you transact your worldly business? I trust, with diligence, whatever your hand findeth to do, doing it with your might; in justice, rendering to all their due, in every circumstance of life; yea, and in mercy, doing unto every man what you would he should do unto you. This is well: But a Christian is called to go still farther,—to add piety to justice; to intermix prayer, especially the prayer of the heart, with all the labour of his hands. Without this, all his diligence and justice only show him to be an honest Heathen; and many there are who profess the Christian religion, that go no farther than honest Heathenism.

Yet again: In what *spirit* do you go through your business? in the spirit of the world, or in the spirit of Christ? I am afraid thousands of those who are called good Christians do not understand the question. If you act in the spirit of Christ, you carry the end you at first proposed through all your work from first to last. You do everything in the spirit of sacrifice, giving up your will to the will of God; and continually aiming, not at ease, pleasure, or riches, not at anything "this short-enduring world can give," but merely at the glory of God. Now, can any one deny, that this is the most excellent way of pursuing worldly business?

Question: How does Wesley recast secular work in the life of the Christian believer? In what ways are we in ministry in our daily work?

Scripture Reflection: Colossians 3:15-17
How does "the word of Christ dwell in you richly" as you live out your daily life?

_____

_____

_____

_____

_____

Day 5 — excerpt from John Wesley's sermon "The More Excellent Way"[19]

Let us consider a little, in what manner the generality of Christians usually converse together. What are the ordinary subjects of their conversation? If it is harmless, (as one would hope it is,) if there be nothing in it profane, nothing immodest, nothing untrue, or unkind; if there be no tale-bearing, backbiting, or evil-speaking, they have reason to praise God for his restraining grace. But there is more than this implied in "ordering our conversation aright." In order to this it is needful, First, that "your communication," that is, discourse or conversation, "be good;" that it be materially good, on good subjects; not fluttering about any thing that occurs; for what have you to do with courts and kings? It is not your business to "Fight o'er the wars, reform the state;" unless when some remarkable event calls for the acknowledgment of the justice or mercy of God. You *must* indeed sometimes talk of worldly things, otherwise we may as well go out of the world. But it should be only so far as is needful: Then we should return to a better subject. Secondly, let your conversation be "to the use of edifying;" calculated to edify either the speaker or the hearers, or both; to build them up, as each has particular need, either in faith, or love, or holiness. Thirdly, see that it not only gives entertainment, but, in one kind or other, "ministers grace to the hearers." Now, is not this "a more excellent way" of conversing than the harmless way above-mentioned?

Question: How does Christian conversation differ from ordinary, casual conversation? How would our conversations change if they were "calculated to edify either the speaker or the hearers, or both"?

Scripture Reflection: John 13:34-35
In what ways would your life change if this commandment of Jesus permeated your life? How would you define a disciple?

_____

_____

_____

_____

Day 6 — excerpt from John Wesley's sermon "The More Excellent Way"[20]

One point only remains to be considered; that is, the use of money. What is the way wherein the generality of Christians employ this? And is there not "a more excellent way?"

The generality of Christians usually set apart something yearly, perhaps a tenth or even one-eighth part of their income, whether it arise from yearly revenue, or from trade, for charitable uses. A few I have known, who said, like Zaccheus, "Lord, the half of my goods I give to the poor." O that it would please God to multiply those friends of mankind, those general benefactors! But,

Besides those who have a stated rule, there are thousands who give large sums to the poor; especially when any striking instance of distress is represented to them in lively colours.

I praise God for all of you who act in this manner. May you never be weary of well-doing! May God restore what you give, seven-fold, into your own bosom! But yet I show unto you "a more excellent way."

You may consider yourself as one in whose hands the Proprietor of heaven and earth, and all things therein, has lodged a part of his goods, to be disposed of according to his direction. And his direction is, that you should look upon yourself as one of a certain number of indigent persons, who are to be provided for out of that portion of his goods wherewith you are entrusted. You have two advantages over the rest: The one, that "it is more blessed to give than to receive;" the other, that you are to serve yourself first, and others afterwards. . . . This was the practice of all the young men at Oxford who were called Methodists. For example: One of them had thirty pounds a year. He lived on twenty-eight, and gave away forty shillings. The next year receiving sixty pounds, he still lived on twenty-eight, and gave away two and thirty. The third year he received ninety pounds, and gave away sixty-two. The fourth year he received a hundred and twenty pounds. Still he lived as before on twenty-eight; and gave to the poor ninety-two. Was not this a more excellent way? . . . As it comes, daily or yearly, so let it go: Otherwise you "lay up treasures upon earth." And this our Lord as flatly forbids as murder and adultery. By doing it, therefore, you would "treasure up to yourselves wrath against the day of wrath and revelation of the righteous judgment of God."

But suppose it were not forbidden, how can you, on principles of reason, spend your money in a way which God may *possibly forgive*, instead of spending it in a manner which he will *certainly reward?* . . .

Who then is a wise man, and endued with knowledge among you? Let him resolve this day, this hour, this moment, the Lord assisting him, to choose in all the preceding particulars the "more excellent way:" And let him steadily keep it, both with regard to sleep, prayer, work, food, conversation, and diversions; and particularly with regard to the employment of that important talent, money. Let *your* heart answer to the call of God, "From this moment, God being my helper, I will lay up no more treasure upon earth: This one thing I will do, I will lay up treasure in heaven; I will render unto God the things that are God's: I will give him all my goods, and all my heart!"

Question: Why is the development of "a more excellent way" in the use of money so important for Christian believers? How do you feel about Wesley's example of the Oxford Methodist (actually Wesley himself)?

Read the session material and make notes in the margins.

_____

_____

_____

_____

_____

Exploration
Background Information: Standards of Christian Conduct

It has been said of the Anglican Church of the eighteenth century that there were really only three rules to follow: believe, behave, and be quiet. It was in opposition to such thinking that John Wesley set in motion the movement that came to be known as Methodism. Wesley was troubled that his church had become so comfortable with itself. The Anglican Church had turned inward, looking to preserve and strengthen itself, ignoring the needs of the community and world. It had no sense of missional or evangelical outreach.

One of the greatest concerns facing Wesley was a theological position that said to people that they could simply believe in God through Jesus Christ and be saved and that their belief required no change in conduct. Although John Wesley never preached anything resembling works righteousness (gaining God's blessing through good acts), he contended that it was impossible to believe in Jesus Christ and continue to live by old standards. Being saved created a new reality, and the new reality called for new rules.

The fundamental rule for John Wesley was that true Christians would live lives of love and service. Belief leads to action. Faith moves us to serve. Christians are doers—people launched into the world in grateful response to what God has done for us.

These issues of Christian conduct moved Wesley from dark pulpits out into the open air. Open-air preaching was frowned upon by the Anglican hierarchy. For Wesley, open-air preaching was necessary to reach the people who needed to hear the gospel. The church did not exist to be served; it existed to serve. The proper conduct of Christians was to love one another in tangible, practical, meaningful ways. Wesley believed that Christian men and women needed to get up off the pews, leave the sanctuaries, and move out into the world.

Discipline

Wesley's concept was disturbing in a society that had worked to create a passive church. Preaching in the early eighteenth century was theologically deep, esoteric, and intellectual. It was "food for thought," but not much else. Church leaders gave little or no consideration to the plight of the poor and needy, the sick, those in prison, or those outside the church. Prayer, fasting, the study of Scripture, and Christian fellowship were domains belonging to the priestly class. The pietism of the seventeenth century found no home in the Anglican Church of Wesley's day. Religion was neatly segmented from the living of daily life.

Throughout his life, John Wesley held to the conviction that practice of the spiritual disciplines would motivate people to active Christian service. Prayer and the study of Scripture would be more than enough to convince people of God's intention for them to move out into the world. As long as the church was the center of Christian learning, individuals would never come to own their personal

Christian vocation. In the Wesleyan movement, small cells—house churches—emerged where people gathered together to pray, to read the Bible, to hold one another accountable for faithful conduct, and to support one another. Discipline became the cornerstone of the early Methodist church.

The Love of God

Beyond discipline, Wesley promoted Christian service. Christian discipline puts us in touch with the will of God. By God's grace we are saved; by faith, we receive God's grace. We can do nothing to earn God's grace, but living in God's grace requires that we share this unconditional gift with others. This distinguished for Wesley what he called "the two orders of Christians." Wesley contended that there are Christians who are satisfied to receive all the blessings that God can give, basking in the warmth of their salvation and holding noble and loving thoughts in their hearts and minds. This is the lower order. The higher order is the Christian who, due to his or her relationship with God, lives out of a condition of grace in which he or she cannot help sharing the love of God with others. For the higher-order Christian, there is no differentiation between the Christian life and ordinary, daily life. The lower-order Christian might be a doctor, a teacher, a lawyer, a foundry worker who happened to believe in Jesus Christ; but the higher-order believer is a Christian doctor, a Christian teacher, a Christian lawyer, or a Christian foundry worker. In all ways, in all things, it is the love of God that sets the tone for living. It is a radical, transforming love that moves people to deep levels of Christian service. In Wesley's view, people demonstrate that love through their conduct.

A Reflective Moment Along the Way

The church's first responsibility is to make disciples. The fourth process of our primary task is to "send persons out into the world in mission." By doing so, we are participating in Wesley's vision of a world transformed one person at a time.

Think about your own discipleship. In what ways do you take your faith "into the world"? Is this a new idea for you?

When your group meets this week, discuss ways your church encourages your members to take their faith "into the world."

What could be done better in our effort to do so? (This question is the final process of our primary task—evaluating for continual improvement.)

Key Concepts for the Journey
Discipleship, Stewardship, and Fellowship

Mainline churches today are poised on the brink of disaster because they have reduced some powerful religious concepts to mere buzzwords. The definition of *buzzword* is "an important-sounding, usually technical word or phrase often of little meaning used chiefly to impress laymen."[21] Three such concepts are discipleship, stewardship, and fellowship.

Discipleship has become the guiding principle for authentic Christian living. To believe in Jesus Christ is to be a disciple. It was not always so. A careful reading of the journals, letters, and sermons of John Wesley reveals that he gave little attention to what we call discipleship. Wesley instructed that we should live Christian lives in holiness. Discipleship was one phase or aspect of that process of Christian living. Discipleship is to the Christian life what childhood and adolescence are to human maturing. Discipleship is a learning and following phase of growth. Discipleship is the period when Christian believers learn fully what following Jesus Christ means.

There is strong biblical precedent for this interpretation of discipleship. In the four gospels, the Twelve Jesus calls are referred to as disciples. After the transformation in the Holy Spirit at Pentecost, the Twelve are never referred to as disciples again. Their followers are known as disciples. Not that any of them ceased to learn and grow in the faith, but their discipleship evolved into something more. They entered a more mature phase of their Christian lives.

Although John Wesley never used the term, what he describes as the mature work of Christians is what we refer to as *stewardship*. Stewardship as a buzzword means little more than raising money to fund the church budget; but in its fullest sense, stewardship is the way we manage all the resources and gifts given

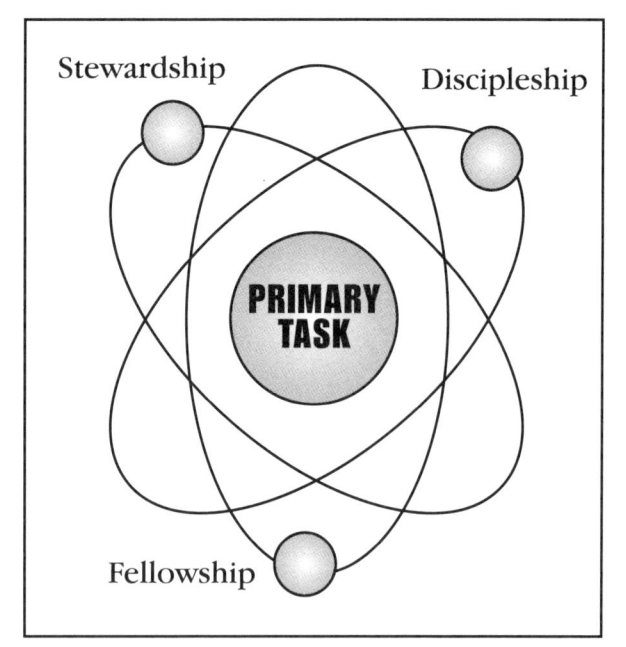

FaithQuest: A New Way of Thinking About the Christian Life

Figure 14A

(Diagram: Stewardship, Discipleship, Fellowship orbiting Primary Task)

to us by God. Discipleship is learning; stewardship is doing. Discipleship is following; stewardship is leading. Discipleship is receiving; stewardship is giving. Discipleship is preparation; stewardship is performance. Today, *discipleship* often takes on the meaning of both stewardship and discipleship, and *stewardship* has been relegated to a lesser position. As people explore the richness of these two concepts, they are beginning to come back into balance. What ultimately creates both balance and power is to reclaim a genuine understanding not only of discipleship and stewardship but of fellowship as well.

Of these three terms, John Wesley speaks only about fellowship with any regularity; and what he means by fellowship is radically different from what we usually mean today.[22] In Wesley's teaching, fellowship is where faith moves from concept to practice. As we connect our faith with the faith of others, we open ourselves to growth. Fellowship is the bridge, the connecting point between discipleship and stewardship. Fellowship is where the abstract and the concrete meet. Fellowship is where Christians gain identity, clarify the mission, and focus on the vision. Christian fellowship witnesses to the world that Christians are different because of their relationship with Jesus Christ. Christians believe certain things and behave in certain ways; and they look for ways to extend the healing, loving mercy of God in Jesus Christ to everyone they meet.

Christians are noticed because they are different. The fellowship of the earliest Christians was remarkable. They operated by different rules. They learned together, they talked together (men and women), they dreamed together, they worked together, and they shared all that they had.

The relationships among *discipleship, stewardship,* and *fellowship* have been lost to The United Methodist Church. Churches today should explore the relationship shared by these three aspects of the Christian life. You will have an opportunity to do this exploration in the Discovery exercise at the end of this session. It is in relationship that these aspects empower us to fulfill our primary task. This relationship also challenges us to look beyond the institutional mission of making disciples to the larger mission of enabling faithful stewards and of creating genuine fellowship.

Questions for Discussion

How do you and other leaders in your church help people develop spiritual disciplines that enable them to grow in their faith?

How have you traditionally defined *discipleship, stewardship,* and *fellowship* in your congregation?

What are you currently doing in your church to develop true stewardship and fellowship?

Discovery
Naming Our Current Reality

Integrating systems for the development of discipleship, stewardship, and fellowship is essential for fulfilling the church's purpose as a disciple-making community. In Figure 14B, examine the ways discipleship, stewardship, and fellowship lay a strong foundation for accomplishing the primary task. How does the primary task provide a framework for

Session 14: The More Excellent Way

PRIMARY TASK OF THE UNITED METHODIST CHURCH

Discipleship
Stewardship
Fellowship

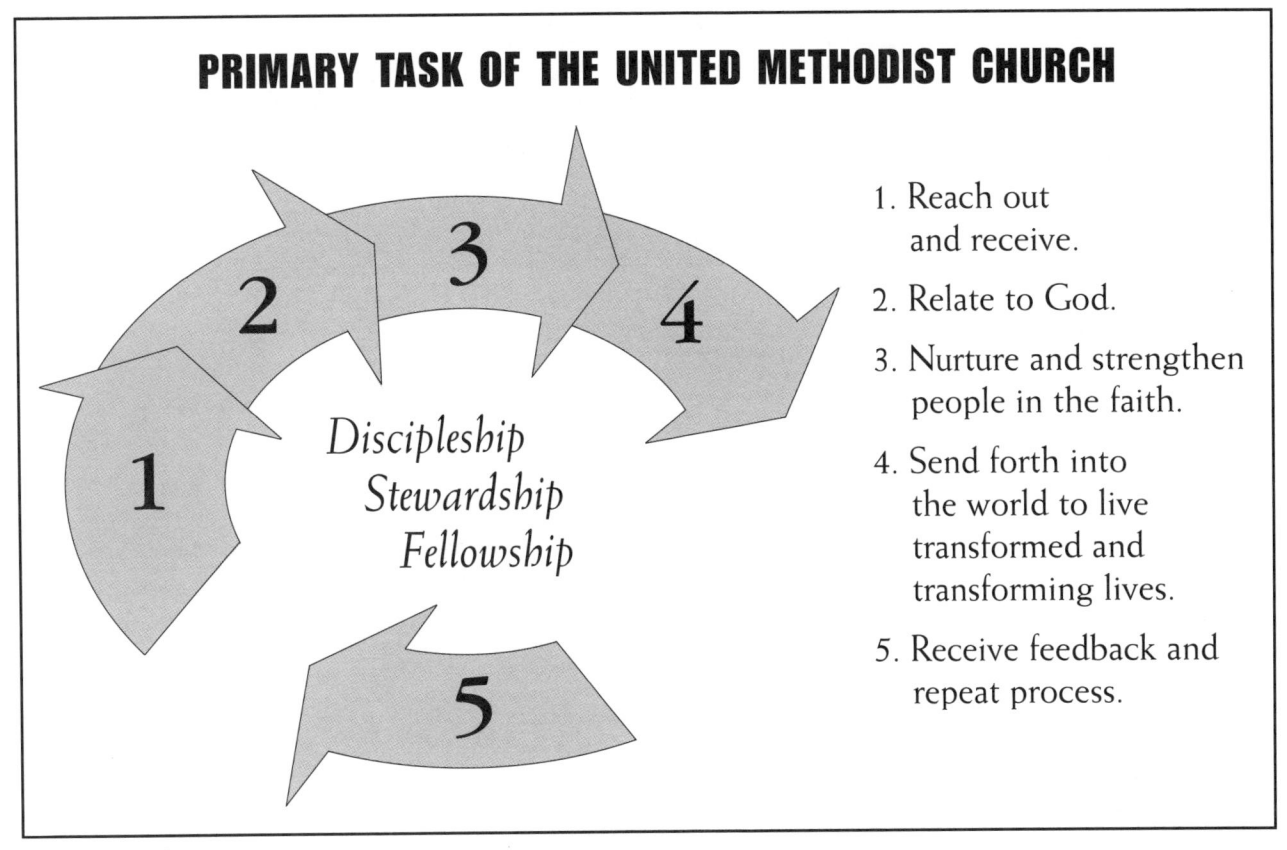

1. Reach out and receive.
2. Relate to God.
3. Nurture and strengthen people in the faith.
4. Send forth into the world to live transformed and transforming lives.
5. Receive feedback and repeat process.

Figure 14B

building discipleship, stewardship, and fellowship systems? What is the symbiotic nature of the relationships? (A symbiotic relationship is one in which two dissimilar organisms or processes combine to accomplish more than either could alone.)

Exercise

Figure 14C helps us think about the ways discipleship, stewardship, fellowship, and the primary task relate. Work through this grid, making notes about the relationship of these concepts and the processes of the primary task.

As you move through the grid, what insights do you receive about the different relationships people have with the church (being more or less active; use of gifts and talents; attitudes toward worship; education; and so on)?

How do the Wesleyan definitions of *discipleship*, *stewardship*, and *fellowship* assist us in moving into the faith-forming-community paradigm?

For Resources, Teaching Aids, and Newest Information

Check out our website at www.faithquest.net.

Figure 14C

	REACH OUT AND RECEIVE	RELATE TO GOD	NURTURE AND STRENGTHEN	SEND FORTH INTO THE WORLD	RETURN AND REPEAT
Discipleship					
Stewardship					
Fellowship					

SESSION 15:
The Means of Grace

Key Wesleyan Concepts:
- The means of grace

Key Concepts for the Journey:
- Clarifying our center
- Values-based community

Outline:
- Gathering
- A Time of Centering
- Prayer
- Preparation
   Questions and Answers
- Exploration
   A Reflective Moment Along the Way
   Questions and Small-Group Exercises
- Discovery
- Conclusion

Introduction

The church exists as the embodiment of Christ in the world. Empowered by the Holy Spirit, the church exists to continue the saving work of Jesus Christ, ushering in the kingdom of God.

What happens when the church gets so busy planning, preparing, and programming that it fails to attend to the basic spiritual needs that provide a foundation? How can we sustain the energy and integrity necessary to be the body of Christ unless we regularly and intentionally return to our spiritual source? It is vital that church leaders stay grounded in the power of God's Holy Spirit. The spiritual health of Christian leaders promotes spiritual health for the entire Christian community.

John Wesley encouraged Methodists to practice the means of grace as a way to place themselves in the path of God's Spirit and power. Congregational leaders should strive to reexamine their spiritual centers and to practice the means of grace faithfully.

Prayer

Almighty and all-loving God, the world demands so much from us that we find ourselves distracted from the important things of this life—our relationships with you and others. Time is such a precious commodity, and we find that we seldom have as much as we would like. When time is limited, often our spiritual well-being suffers most. Help us to be disciplined in our attention to matters of the heart and spirit. Empower us to make time for the things that benefit us most, and help us to grow into the likeness of Jesus Christ, our Savior and our Lord. Amen.

Preparation
Daily Reading and Questions for Reflection

Day 1 — excerpt from John Wesley's sermon "The Means of Grace"[23]

But are there any *ordinances* now, since life and immortality were brought to light by the gospel? Are there, under the Christian dispensation, any *means ordained* of God, as the usual channels of his grace? This question could never have been proposed in the apostolical church, unless by one who openly avowed himself to be a Heathen; the whole body of Christians being agreed, that Christ had ordained certain outward means, for conveying his grace into the souls of men. Their constant practice set this beyond all dispute; for so long as "all that believed were together, and had all things common," (Acts ii.44,) "they continued steadfastly in the teaching of the Apostles, and in breaking of bread, and in prayers." (Verse 42.)

But in process of time, when "the love of many waxed cold," some began to mistake the *means* for the *end*, and to place religion rather in doing those outward works, than in a heart renewed after the image of God. They forgot that "the end of" every "commandment is love, out of a pure heart," with "faith unfeigned;" the loving the Lord their God with all their heart, and their neighbour as themselves; and the being purified from pride, anger, and evil desire, by a "faith of the operation of God." Others seemed to imagine, that though religion did not principally consist in these outward means, yet there was something in them wherewith God was well pleased; something that would still make them acceptable in his sight, though they were not exact in the weightier matters of the law, in justice, mercy, and the love of God. ...

In the following discourse, I propose to examine at large, whether there are any means of grace.

By "means of grace" I understand outward signs, words, or actions, ordained of God, and appointed for this end, to be the ordinary channels whereby he might convey to men, preventing, justifying, or sanctifying grace.

I use this expression, means of grace, because I know none better; and because it has been generally used in the Christian Church for many ages,—in particular by our own Church, which directs us to bless God both for the means of grace, and hope of glory; and teaches us, that a sacrament is "an outward sign of inward grace, and a means whereby we receive the same."

The chief of these means are prayer, whether in secret or with the great congregation; searching the Scriptures; (which implies reading, hearing, and meditating thereon;) and receiving the Lord's supper, eating bread and drinking wine in remembrance of Him: And these we believe to be ordained of God, as the ordinary channels of conveying his grace to the souls of men.

Question: What do you understand the phrase "means of grace" to mean? Can you think of other means of grace beyond those identified by Wesley?

Scripture Reflection: Acts 2:43-47
What means of grace can you identify in this passage from the Book of Acts?

Day 2 — excerpt from John Wesley's sermon "The Means of Grace"[24]

But we allow, that the whole value of the means depends on their actual subservience to the end of religion; that, consequently, all these means, when separate from the end, are less than nothing and vanity; that if they do not actually conduce to the knowledge and love of God, they are not acceptable in his sight; yea, rather, they are an abomination before him, a stink in his nostrils; he is weary to bear them. Above all, if they are used as a kind of *commutation* for the religion they were designed to subserve, it is not easy to find words for the enormous folly and wickedness of thus turning God's arms against himself; of keeping Christianity out of the heart by those very means which were ordained for the bringing it in.

We allow, likewise, that all outward means whatever, if separate from the Spirit of God, cannot profit at all, cannot conduce, in any degree, either to the knowledge or love of God. Without controversy, the help that is done upon earth, He doeth it himself. It is He alone who, by his own almighty power, worketh in us what is pleasing in his sight; and all outward things, unless He work in them and by them, are mere weak and beggarly elements. Whosoever, therefore, imagines there is any intrinsic power in any means whatsoever, does greatly err, not knowing the Scriptures, neither the power of God. We know that there is no inherent power in the words that are spoken in prayer, in the letter of Scripture read, the sound thereof heard, or the bread and wine received in the Lord's supper; but that it is God alone who is the Giver of every good gift, the Author of all grace; that the whole power is of Him, whereby, through any of these, there is any blessing conveyed to our souls. We know, likewise, that he is able to give the same grace, though there were no means on the face of the earth. In this sense, we may affirm, that, with regard to God, there is no such thing as means; seeing he is equally able to work whatsoever pleaseth him, by any, or by none at all.

We allow farther, that the use of all means whatever will never atone for one sin; that it is the blood of Christ alone, whereby any sinner can be reconciled to God; there being no other propitiation for our sins, no other fountain for sin and uncleanness. Every believer in Christ is deeply convinced that there is no merit but in Him; that there is no merit in any of his own works; not in uttering the prayer, or searching the Scripture, or hearing the word of God, or eating of that bread and drinking of that cup. So that if no more be intended by the expression some have used, "Christ is the only means of grace," than this,—that He is the only meritorious cause of it, it cannot be gainsayed by any who know the grace of God.

Question: Given that all that Wesley says in this reading is true, what profit is there in practicing the means of grace?

Scripture Reflection: Matthew 6:19-21
Does Wesley speak of the means of grace above as treasures to be laid up? In what way yes or no?

_____

_____

_____

_____

_____

Day 3 — excerpt from John Wesley's sermon "The Means of Grace"[25]

According to this, according to the decision of holy writ, all who desire the grace of God are to wait for it in the means which he hath ordained; in using, not in laying them aside.

And, First, all who desire the grace of God are to wait for it in the way of prayer. This is the express direction of our Lord himself. In his Sermon upon the Mount, after explaining at large wherein religion consists, and describing the main branches of it, he adds, "Ask, and it shall be given you; seek, and ye shall find; knock, and it shall be opened unto you: For every one that asketh receiveth; and he that seeketh findeth; and to him that knocketh it shall be opened." (Matt. vii.7, 8.) Here we are in the plainest manner directed to ask, in order to, or as a means of, receiving; to seek, in order to find, the grace of God, the pearl of great price; and to knock, to continue asking and seeking, if we would enter into his kingdom....

The absolute necessity of using this means, if we would receive any gift from God, yet farther appears from that remarkable passage which immediately precedes these words: "And he said unto them," whom he had just been teaching how to pray, "Which of you shall have a friend, and shall go unto him at midnight, and shall say unto him, Friend, lend me three loaves: And he from within shall answer, Trouble me not; I cannot rise and give thee. I say unto you, though he will not rise and give him, because he is his friend, yet because of his importunity, he will rise, and give him as many as he needeth. And I say unto you, Ask, and it shall be given you." (Luke xi.5, 7-9.) "Though he will not give him, because he is his friend, yet because of his importunity he will rise and give him as many as he needeth." How could our blessed Lord more plainly declare, that we may receive of God, by this means, by importunately asking, what otherwise we should not receive at all?

"He spake also another parable, to this end, that men ought always to pray, and not to faint," till through this means they should receive of God whatsoever petition they asked of him: "There was in a city a judge which feared not God, neither regarded man. And there was a widow in that city, and she came unto him, saying, Avenge me of my adversary. And he would not for a while; but afterwards he said within himself, Though I fear not God, nor regard man, yet because this widow troubleth me, I will avenge her, lest, by her continual coming, she weary me." (Luke xviii.1-5.) The application of this our Lord himself hath made: "Hear what the unjust judge saith!" Because she continues to ask, because she will take no denial, therefore I will avenge her. "And shall not God avenge his own elect, which cry day and night unto him? I tell you he will avenge them speedily," if they pray and faint not.

Question: What are the qualities of prayer that Wesley describes? How is prayer experienced and practiced in your congregation?

FaithQuest: A New Way of Thinking About the Christian Life

Scripture Reflection: Luke 11:5-10

Our culture is used to instant gratification of our needs. What might Wesley, or for that matter, Jesus, have to say to us today regarding prayer?

_____

_____

_____

_____

_____

_____

Scripture Reflection: 2 Timothy 3:14-17

Wesley refers to this text when he speaks above about Scripture being inspired by God. What does this teaching mean for your own journey of faith?

_____

_____

_____

_____

_____

_____

Day 4 — excerpt from John Wesley's sermon "The Means of Grace"[26]

Secondly. All who desire the grace of God are to wait for it in searching the Scriptures.

Our Lord's direction, with regard to the use of this means, is likewise plain and clear. "Search the Scriptures," saith he to the unbelieving Jews, "for they testify of me." (John v.39.) And for this very end did he direct them to search the Scriptures, that they might believe in him....

And that this is a means whereby God not only gives, but also confirms and increases, true wisdom, we learn from the words of St. Paul to Timothy: "From a child thou hast known the Holy Scriptures, which are able to make thee wise unto salvation through faith which is in Christ Jesus." (2 Tim. iii.15.) The same truth (namely, that this is the great means God has ordained for conveying his manifold grace to man) is delivered, in the fullest manner that can be conceived, in the words which immediately follow: "All Scripture is given by inspiration of God," consequently, all Scripture is infallibly true; "and is profitable for doctrine, for reproof, for correction, for instruction in righteousness;" to the end "that the man of God may be perfect, thoroughly furnished unto all good works."

Question: How does "searching the Scriptures" differ from "reading the Bible"? What opportunities for "searching the Scriptures" (in the Wesleyan meaning) are available to you and members of your congregation?

Day 5 — excerpt from John Wesley's sermon "The Means of Grace"[27]

Thirdly. All who desire an increase of the grace of God are to wait for it in partaking of the Lord's supper: For this also is a direction himself hath given. "The same night in which he was betrayed, he took bread, and brake it, and said, Take, eat; this is my body;" that is, the sacred sign of my body: "This do in remembrance of me." Likewise, "he took the cup, saying, This cup is the new testament," or covenant: ... "this do ye in remembrance of me." "For as often as ye eat this bread, and drink this cup, ye do show forth the Lord's death till he come:" (1 Cor. xi.23, &c.:) Ye openly exhibit the same, by these visible signs, before God, and angels, and men; ye manifest your solemn remembrance of his death, till he cometh in the clouds of heaven....

And that this is also an ordinary, stated means of receiving the grace of God, is evident from those words of the Apostle, which occur in the preceding chapter: "The cup of blessing which we bless, is it not the communion," or *communication*, "of the blood of Christ? The bread which we break, is it not the communion of the body of Christ?" (1 Cor. x.16.) Is not the eating of that bread, and the drinking of that cup, the outward, visible means, whereby God conveys into our souls all that spiritual grace, that righteousness, and peace, and joy in the Holy Ghost, which were purchased by the body of Christ once broken and the blood of Christ once shed for us? Let all, therefore, who truly desire the grace of God, eat of that bread, and drink of that cup.

Question: In what ways does viewing the Lord's Supper as a means of grace define, clarify, or challenge your understanding of Communion?

Scripture Reflection: Luke 22:19-20
There was a time in our history when Holy Communion was celebrated infrequently. What might Wesley have said about such a tradition? Is the frequency of this celebration changing in your congregation today?

_____
_____
_____
_____
_____

Day 6 — excerpt from John Wesley's sermon "The Means of Grace"[28]

But this being allowed, that all who desire the grace of God are to wait for it in the means he hath ordained; it may still be inquired, how those means should be used, both as to the order and the manner of using them.

...And in the mean time, the sure and general rule for all who groan for the salvation of God is this,—whenever opportunity serves, use all the means which God has ordained; for who knows in which God will meet thee with the grace that bringeth salvation?

As to the manner of using them, whereon indeed it wholly depends whether they shall convey any grace at all to the user; it behoves us, First, always to retain a lively sense, that God is above all means. Have a care, therefore, of limiting the Almighty. He doeth whatsoever and whensoever it pleaseth him. He can convey his grace, either in or out of any of the means which he hath appointed. Perhaps he will. "Who hath known the mind of the Lord? or who hath been his counsellor?" Look then every moment for his appearing! Be it at the hour you are employed in his ordinances; or before, or after that hour; or when you are hindered therefrom. He is not hindered; He is always ready, always able, always willing to save. "It is the Lord: Let him do what seemeth him good!"

Secondly. Before you use any means, let it be deeply impressed on your soul,—there is no *power* in this. It is, in itself, a poor, dead, empty thing: Separate from God, it is a dry leaf, a shadow. Neither is there any *merit* in my using this; nothing intrinsically pleasing to God; nothing whereby I deserve any favour at his hands, no, not a drop of water to cool my tongue. But, because God bids, therefore I do; because he directs me to wait in this way, therefore here I wait for his free mercy, whereof cometh my salvation.

Settle this in your heart, that the *opus operatum*, the mere *work done*, profiteth nothing; that there is no *power* to save, but in the Spirit of God, no *merit*, but in the blood of Christ; that, consequently, even what God ordains, conveys no grace to the soul, if you trust not in Him alone. On the other hand, he that does truly trust in Him, cannot fall short of the grace of God, even though he were cut off from every outward ordinance, though he were shut up in the centre of the earth.

Thirdly. In using all means, seek God alone. In and through every outward thing, look singly to the *power* of his Spirit, and the *merits* of his Son. Beware you do not stick in the *work* itself; if you do, it is all lost labour. Nothing short of God can satisfy your soul. Therefore, eye him in all, through all, and above all.

Question: Why does Wesley emphasize that there is no power or merit in the means of grace themselves? What is the danger in believing otherwise?

Read the session material and make notes in the margins.

_____
_____
_____
_____
_____

Exploration
Background Information: The Means of Grace

When you hear the phrase "the means of grace," what comes to mind? Throughout the history of the Christian church, different religious leaders in different places have referred to the means of God's grace. Means of grace are the practices that enable Christians to be more receptive to the grace of God. The list of the means of grace may vary, but the intent is the same.

The means of grace are not ways of *earning* God's forgiveness or mercy. God gives grace as God wills. We can do nothing to warrant God's saving love. The means of grace are not works righteousness. Instead, they prepare us to recognize the grace of God in the many ways God reveals it to us throughout our lives. God's grace is bountiful. God makes forgiveness, mercy, and love available to us in many different ways. When we are not "tuned in" to it, we miss many wonderful occasions for reconciliation.

Over the course of his ministry, John Wesley named many "means of grace." Henry H. Knight III identifies seventeen different classifications of the means of grace in Wesley's sermons and writings.[29] Knight further divides the means of grace into three subtypes: general, instituted, and prudential. Although Wesley mentioned different means in different situations, three of the means of grace remained constant from his earliest ministry until the day he died: prayer, study of Scripture, and attendance at the Lord's Supper. For Wesley, there was no better way to meet God than to engage in these regular disciplines of the Spirit.

Beyond these three fundamental practices, Wesley often spoke of the need for Christian conference as a means of grace. What Wesley meant by this quaint phrase was the regular, intentional participation in conversation centered in faith-sharing and mutual accountability. By talking about the faith with other believers, objectivity was achieved, and the grace of God often emerged.

Another means of grace that Wesley proclaimed regularly in his later years was acts of mercy. According to Wesley, the ground of God's grace is God's love. Love is fundamental to all the means of grace, and love must be active. Love must move us into service to those in need. Acts of mercy move us fully into the love of God.

At one time or another, Wesley cited all the classical spiritual disciplines as means of God's grace. The actual practice of the spiritual disciplines was less important than the intention of the heart—the perpetual seeking of God in the believer's life. When men and women are faithful to seek God, God is faithful to be found. The means of grace increase our receptivity to discovering God's grace in our lives.

A Reflective Moment Along the Way

It is noted above that Wesley believed in particular that three of the means of grace were especially important to our growing and maturing in faith and love. These, again, were prayer, the study of Scripture, and participating in the Lord's Supper.

Consider how these three ways of experiencing God have operated in your life. Over the past weeks, your group has become a newly-formed faith community. Prepare to talk with one another about how each of these means of grace has been a part of your life. Conclude this reflective moment by reading, in unison, the prayer at the beginning of this session.

Key Concepts for the Journey
Clarifying Our Center

The sign in front of a Nashville Taco Bell proudly proclaims, "We Sell Tacos!" Although this seems obvious, it helps us know what to expect when we enter the doors of Taco Bell. Is the same true of our churches? The sign in front of the church might identify us by name, but what does the banner beneath it proclaim? What do people assume they will find when they enter?

A twenty-something woman from Illinois said recently, "I visited the church in our neighborhood. I entered a side door and found myself in a thrift shop. I walked down the hall and interrupted a twelve-step group. I passed step aerobics, a building committee meeting, and a seniors' luncheon. I stopped and chatted with some women making crafts. I exited the building through a children's play group and went home. My husband asked me where I went that day. I told him, 'I'm not sure.'"

When people leave our church buildings, have they been to church? Do people really know what we are all about after they visit us? It is not the responsibility of people who visit our churches to figure out what we're all about. It is the responsibility of the leadership of the local congregation to make it clear what the church has to offer. No one should leave a congregation confused. Our churches are places where people come together to meet God. This is the one thing we should offer better than anyone else. It is the reason we exist.

Although we spend a lot of time in our local churches clarifying the work we do, we often do not spend enough time clarifying our center—focusing on Christ, who defines our work and our service to the world. We must be careful not to get so wrapped up in leading the church that we forget to follow the Christ. Often, the most important work we can do for the church is to step back and do nothing; just wait, listen, reflect, and pray. Before we plan, we need to prepare. Practicing the means of grace is an excellent way to prepare for effective leadership. Attending to God in prayer, study, Communion, fasting, Christian conversation, and the like opens us to the vision that God wants to unfold. We are better leaders when we are faithful followers. We need to ask ourselves, "How deep is the well from which we draw? How firmly rooted are we in the source of our spiritual power? How closely tied to God are we? Does our work reflect the nature of our relationship with God? How well do we model discipleship and faithful Christian living so that our words carry the weight that can transform lives?" If we neglect our spiritual health, we will have nothing of value to offer.

Values-Based Community

Ask people in your congregation why they come to church. The answers they give will probably concern relationships. Even when they say they come for the choir, or for the Bible study, or for the worship, their underlying desire is to be in relationship with God or other people. Virtually no one will say that he or she comes to church to work on a committee, to accomplish a task, or to plan programs. The vast majority of people in church are seeking community and connection.

People seek connection and community in the church because they believe that the church offers an important alternative to the predominant culture. What does the church offer that people find nowhere else? Beyond Jesus Christ, the answer is a set of values and attributes that define the church as something special—values such as love, hope, charity, justice, mercy, and honesty; attributes such as compassion, kindness, peace, generosity, patience, and forgiveness. The church offers us the possibility of living a different kind of life. Qualities that are difficult to maintain in the day-to-day world are reinforced and strengthened in Christian community. Many people search for a bastion of moral decency and integrity, so they turn to the church. How disappointing it must be to discover that many churches are not focusing on core values, but instead are concentrating on programs and planning. Many churches are so busy doing church work that they have no time to be the church.

A group of seventy-four clergy and laypeople from the Southeastern Jurisdiction of The United Methodist Church were asked to list the three most important values upon which our church is based. Eighty-one different values were listed, with only four (love, kindness, caring, and friendliness) being named ten or more times. With such a clear lack of consensus about the core values of The United Methodist Church, how can we be sure that people leave our churches with clarity about who we are and what we believe? Even before we examine our mission and cast a vision for ministry, we need to spend time discussing and understanding the core values upon which we base our ministry. People are attracted to values-based communities. People are seeking centers of support and acceptance where they can safely struggle with issues of morality and right conduct. The values that Jesus, Paul, and John Wesley loudly proclaimed create a safe space where no one is judged, no one is condemned, everyone is welcome, and no one lacks for anything. The church that is centered in solid Christian values celebrates diversity, welcomes challenge, and opens its arms to receive everyone. Love is the rule of the values-based Christian community. Truly, this is different from what the predominant culture has to offer.

Long before structures are set in place, long before committees are formed and people are elected to lead, long before mission and vision statements are drafted, the important process of examining core values needs to take place. Practicing the Wesleyan means of grace is an excellent way to gain focus. In prayer, the study of Scripture, celebrating Communion, and deep, meaningful Christian conversation, shared values come to light.

Questions for Discussion

How much of your committee, organization, and planning time is devoted to clarifying your central focus on Jesus and centering on your relationship with God? How can you devote more time to creating community and less time to attending committee meetings?

When people outside your church fellowship enter your meetings, activities, and functions, do they really know they are in the church or might it be confused with another goodwill community group?

FaithQuest: A New Way of Thinking About the Christian Life

What are the core values upon which you base your ministry and your life together? How do you communicate these values?

_____

_____

_____

_____

_____

Discovery
Naming Our Current Reality

Many churches begin meetings with a short devotional time. Someone offers words of encouragement, a Scripture reading, a hymn, and a prayer; then the meeting proceeds. At times, the devotion is a perfunctory obligation to get out of the way so that the "real" work can take place. At other times, the devotion is just one more agenda item on a long, long list. Either way, the devotion loses its power to set the tone of the work. Instead of viewing the devotion as one element of a ninety-minute meeting, consider the work you do as part of a ninety-minute time of devotion. This is often referred to as worshipful work. This perception would change your approach to ministry.

Exercise

In session one, we identified the paradigm shift from the activity-center model to the faith-forming-community model based on spiritual disciplines and the practice of the means of grace. Look at Figure 15A. How do we break open the activity-center model on the left so that we might focus on the list on the right? (You may need to change the committee list on the left to match your congregation's structure.) Once we focus on the means of grace, what structures will we need to ensure their ongoing practice?

Does one list necessarily exclude the other? What needs to change in the congregation to make sure that both appropriate structures for ministry *and* the means of grace are kept in proper balance?

_____

_____

_____

_____

_____

_____

For Resources, Teaching Aids, and Newest Information

Check out our website at www.faithquest.net.

Figure 15A

CHURCH AS ACTIVITY CENTER	CHURCH AS FAITH-FORMING COMMUNITY
Worship Committee	Prayer
Christian Education Committee	Study of Scripture
Stewardship Task Force	Lord's Supper
Evangelism Committee	Fasting
Missions Work Area	Acts of Mercy
Membership Committee	Christian Conference
Church and Society Work Area	

SESSION 16:
To Spread Scriptural Holiness Across the Land

Key Wesleyan Concepts:
- Justification and personal holiness
- Corporate holiness and the kingdom of God

Key Concepts for the Journey:
- Quality versus excellence
- Empowerment

Outline:
- Gathering
- A Time of Centering
- Prayer
- Preparation
    Questions and Answers
- Exploration
    A Reflective Moment Along the Way
    Questions and Small-Group Exercises
- Discovery
- Conclusion

Introduction

What does it really mean to be a Christian? Are Christians to live by standards different from those of non-Christians? Is there a verifiable difference in the way that Christians and non-Christians act?

Everyone assumes that to be Christian means to be different. Most Christians are aware of the benefits they receive from a strong and abiding faith. Once saved, we have the promise of the forgiveness of sins and eternal life. All too often, Christian men and women rest upon the blessings received, without experiencing a fundamental change in the way they move through the world. John Wesley encouraged and proclaimed personal and corporate holiness as the responsibility of those calling themselves Christian. In Wesley's view, it is impossible to live in the sanctifying grace of God and not behave in a holy and loving way.

Prayer

Gracious and loving God, help us to take time to examine ourselves in the light of your love. Without guilt, without personal condemnation, enable us to see the places of weakness in our lives. Reveal the areas of our lives that we hold in reserve from you, choosing to live our way instead of yours. Open us to hear your word with new ears, and open our hearts to the desire to please you with every thought we have, every word we utter, and every action we take. Break through the worldly crust to disclose our heavenly core, we pray in Jesus' name. Amen.

Preparation
Daily Reading and Questions for Reflection

Day 1 — excerpt from John Wesley's sermon "The Circumcision of the Heart"[30]

It is the melancholy remark of an excellent man, that he who now preaches the most essential duties of Christianity, runs the hazard of being esteemed, by a great part of his hearers, "a setter forth of new doctrines." Most men have so *lived away* the substance of that religion, the profession whereof they still retain, that no sooner are any of those truths proposed which difference the Spirit of Christ from the spirit of the world, than they cry out, "Thou bringest strange things to our ears; we would know what these things mean:"—Though he is only preaching to them "Jesus and the resurrection," with the necessary consequence of it,—If Christ be risen, ye ought then to die unto the world, and to live wholly unto God....

That "circumcision is that of the heart, in the spirit, and not in the letter;"—that the distinguishing mark of a true follower of Christ, of one who is in a state of acceptance with God, is not either outward circumcision, or baptism, or any other outward form, but a right state of soul, a mind and spirit renewed after the image of Him that created it;—is one of those important truths that can only be spiritually discerned.... Know that the circumcision of the heart, the seal of thy calling, is foolishness with the world. Be content to wait for thy applause till the day of thy Lord's appearing. In that day shalt thou have praise of God, in the great assembly of men and angels.

Question: What is the "circumcision of the heart"? (See Acts 15:1-11 for help.) What do you think Wesley means when he calls the circumcision of the heart the "seal of thy calling"?

Scripture Reflection: Ephesians 1:11-14
In a day when promises don't seem to mean very much, what this does passage say to us about God? What sustains our relationship with God on a daily basis?

_____

_____

_____

_____

_____

Day 2 — excerpt from John Wesley's sermon "The Circumcision of the Heart"[31]

I am, First, to inquire, wherein that circumcision of the heart consists, which will receive the praise of God. In general we may observe, it is that habitual disposition of soul which, in the sacred writings, is termed holiness; and which directly implies, the being cleansed from sin, "from all filthiness both of flesh and spirit;" and, by consequence, the being endued with those virtues which were also in Christ Jesus; the being so "renewed in the spirit of our mind," as to be "perfect as our Father in heaven is perfect."

To be more particular: Circumcision of heart implies humility, faith, hope, and charity. Humility, a right judgment of ourselves, cleanses our minds from those high conceits of our own perfections, from that undue opinion of our own abilities and attainments, which are the genuine fruit of a corrupted nature. This entirely cuts off that vain thought, "I am rich, and wise, and have need of nothing;" and convinces us that we are by nature "wretched, and poor, and miserable, and blind, and naked." It convinces us, that in our best estate we are, of ourselves, all sin and vanity; that confusion, and ignorance, and error reign over our understanding; that unreasonable, earthly, sensual, devilish passions usurp authority over our will; in a word, that there is no whole part in our soul, that all the foundations of our nature are out of course.

At the same time we are convinced, that we are not sufficient of ourselves to help ourselves; that, without the Spirit of God, we can do nothing but add sin to sin; that it is He alone who worketh in us by his almighty power, either to will or do that which is good; it being as impossible for us even to think a good thought, without the supernatural assistance of his Spirit, as to create ourselves, or to renew our whole souls in righteousness and true holiness.

A sure effect of our having formed this right judgment of the sinfulness and helplessness of our nature, is a disregard of that "honour which cometh of man," which is usually paid to some supposed excellency in us. He who knows himself, neither desires nor values the applause which he knows he deserves not. It is therefore "a very small thing with him, to be judged by man's judgment." He has all reason to think, by comparing what it has said, either for or against him, with what he feels in his own breast, that the world, as well as the god of this world, was "a liar from the beginning." And even as to those who are not of the world; though he would choose, if it were the will of God, that they should account of him as of one desirous to be found a faithful steward of his Lord's goods, if haply this might be a means of enabling him to be of more use to his fellow-servants, yet as this is the one end of his wishing for their approbation, so he does not at all rest upon it: For he is assured, that whatever God wills, he can never want instruments to perform; since he is able, even of these stones, to raise up servants to do his pleasure.

Question: Why is humility set as the cornerstone for a life of holiness and service to God?

Scripture Reflection: 1 Peter 5:5-6
How is humility encouraged in your congregation? Is there a relationship between being a welcoming community of faith and living in the realm of humility?

_____

_____

_____

_____

_____

Day 3 — excerpt from John Wesley's sermon "The Circumcision of the Heart"[32]

The best guide of the blind, the surest light of them that are in darkness, the most perfect instructor of the foolish, is faith. But it must be such a faith as is "mighty through God, to the pulling down of strong-holds,"—to the overturning all the prejudices of corrupt reason, all the false maxims revered among men, all evil customs and habits, all that "wisdom of the world which is foolishness with God;" as "casteth down imaginations," reasonings, "and every high thing that exalteth itself against the knowledge of God, and bringeth into captivity every thought to the obedience of Christ."

..."This is the victory which overcometh the world, even our faith;" that faith, which is not only an unshaken assent to all that God hath revealed in Scripture,—and in particular to those important truths, "Jesus Christ came into the world to save sinners;" "He bare our sins in his own body on the tree;" "He is the propitiation for our sins, and not for ours only, but also for the sins of the whole world;"—but likewise the revelation of Christ in our hearts; a divine evidence or conviction of his love, his free, unmerited love to me a sinner; a sure confidence in his pardoning mercy, wrought in us by the Holy Ghost; a confidence, whereby every true believer is enabled to bear witness, "I know that my Redeemer liveth," that I have an "Advocate with the Father," and that "Jesus Christ the righteous" is my Lord, and "the propitiation for my sins,"—I know he hath "loved me, and given himself for me,"—He hath reconciled me, even me, to God; and I "have redemption through his blood, even the forgiveness of sins."

Question: How would you explain Wesley's understanding of faith to someone else (using your own words)? How does Wesley's understanding of faith compare to your own?

Scripture Reflection: Hebrews 11:1-3, 6
How does Wesley's understanding of faith compare with that of the author of the Letter to the Hebrews?

_____

_____

_____

_____

_____

_____

Day 4 — excerpt from John Wesley's sermon "The Circumcision of the Heart"[33]

Those who are thus by faith born of God, have also strong consolation through hope. This is the next thing which the circumcision of the heart implies; even the testimony of their own spirit with the Spirit which witnesses in their hearts that they are the children of God. Indeed it is the same Spirit who works in them that clear and cheerful confidence that their heart is upright toward God; that good assurance, that they now do, through his grace, the things which are acceptable in his sight; that they are now in the path which leadeth to life, and shall, by the mercy of God, endure therein to the end. It is He who giveth them a lively expectation of receiving all good things at God's hand; a joyous prospect of that crown of glory, which is reserved in heaven for them. By this anchor a Christian is kept steady in the midst of the waves of this troublesome world, and preserved from striking upon either of those fatal rocks,—presumption or despair. He is neither discouraged by the misconceived severity of his Lord, nor does he "despise the richness of his goodness." He neither apprehends the difficulties of the race set before him to be greater than he has strength to conquer, nor expects them to be so little as to yield in the conquest, till he has put forth all his strength. The experience he already has in the Christian warfare, as it assures him his "labour is not in vain" if "whatever his hand findeth to do, he doeth it with his might;" so it forbids his entertaining so vain a thought, as that he can otherwise gain any advantage, as that any virtue can be shown, any praise attained, by faint hearts and feeble hands; or, indeed, by any but those who pursue the same course with the great Apostle of the Gentiles: "I," says he, "so run, not as uncertainly; so fight I, not as one that beateth the air: But I keep under my body, and bring it into subjection; lest, by any means, when I have preached to others, I myself should be a castaway."

Question: Where do you experience hope in your life? How are people encouraged in hope in your church? How do you discover what people most deeply hope for?

Scripture Reflection: Psalm 146

The Psalmist is expressing God's vision of a righteous and just world. How do hope and justice relate to each other in the life of the church as a faith-forming community?

_____

_____

_____

_____

Day 5 — excerpt from John Wesley's sermon "The Circumcision of the Heart"[34]

Yet lackest thou one thing, whosoever thou art, that to a deep humility, and a steadfast faith, hast joined a lively hope, and thereby in a good measure cleansed thy heart from its inbred pollution. If thou wilt be perfect, add to all these, charity; add love, and thou hast the circumcision of the heart. "Love is the fulfilling of the law, the end of the commandment." Very excellent things are spoken of love; it is the essence, the spirit, the life of all virtue. It is not only the first and great command, but it is all the commandments in one. "Whatsoever things are just, whatsoever things are pure, whatsoever things are amiable," or honourable; "if there be any virtue, if there be any praise," they are all comprised in this one word,—love. In this is perfection, and glory, and happiness. The royal law of heaven and earth is this, "Thou shalt love the Lord thy God with all thy heart, and with all thy soul, and with all thy mind, and with all thy strength." . . .

Have no end, no ultimate end, but God. Thus our Lord: "One thing is needful." And if thine eye be singly fixed on this one thing, "thy whole body shall be full of light." Thus St. Paul: "This one thing I do; I press toward the mark, for the prize of the high calling in Christ Jesus." Thus St. James: "Cleanse your hands, ye sinners, and purify your hearts, ye double-minded." Thus St. John: "Love not the world, neither the things that are in the world. For all that is in the world, the lust of the flesh, the lust of the eye, and the pride of life, is not of the Father, but is of the world." The seeking happiness in what gratifies either the desire of the flesh, by agreeably striking upon the outward senses; the desire of the eye, of the imagination, by its novelty, greatness, or beauty; or the pride of life, whether by pomp, grandeur, power, or, the usual consequence of them, applause and admiration;—"is not of the Father," cometh not from, neither is approved by, the Father of spirits; "but of the world." It is the distinguishing mark of those who will not have Him to reign over them.

Question: In what ways are you growing in love for God, for self, and for neighbor? How does your Christian community facilitate growth in love?

Scripture Reflection: 1 Corinthians 13:1-7, 13
These are beautiful words. How might the church use these words to help people understand that all Christians are called into the process of "becoming" what God would have them become?

_____

_____

_____

_____

_____

Day 6 — excerpt from John Wesley's sermon "The Circumcision of the Heart"[35]

Here, then, is the sum of the perfect law; this is the true circumcision of the heart. Let the spirit return to God that gave it, with the whole train of its affections. "Unto the place from whence all the rivers came," thither let them flow again. Other sacrifices from us he would not; but the living sacrifice of the heart he hath chosen. Let it be continually offered up to God through Christ, in flames of holy love. And let no creature be suffered to share with him: For he is a jealous God. His throne will he not divide with another: He will reign without a rival. Be no design, no desire admitted there, but what has Him for its ultimate object. This is the way wherein those children of God once walked, who, being dead, still speak to us: "Desire not to live, but to praise his name: Let all your thoughts, words, and works tend to his glory. Set your heart firm on him, and on other things only as they are in and from him. Let your soul be filled with so entire a love of him, that you may love nothing but for his sake." "Have a pure intention of heart, a steadfast regard to his glory in all your actions." "Fix your eye upon the blessed hope of your calling, and make all the things of the world minister unto it." For then, and not till then, is that "mind in us which was also in Christ Jesus;" when, in every motion of our heart, in every word of our tongue, in every work of our hands, we "pursue nothing but in relation to him, and in subordination to his pleasure;" when we, too, neither think, nor speak, nor act, to fulfill our "own will, but the will of him that sent us;" when, whether we "eat, or drink, or whatever we do, we do all to the glory of God."

Question: According to Wesley, what is the ultimate goal and purpose of the Christian life?

Read the session material and make notes in the margins.

_____

_____

_____

_____

_____

_____

Exploration
Background Information: Justification and Personal Holiness

Justification by faith has been the subject of theological thought and debate for centuries. The apostle Paul spoke of justification in the Letter to the Romans. In its simplest form, *justification* means that we have been made acceptable to God through the atoning sacrifice of Jesus Christ on the cross. Jesus does for us what we cannot do for ourselves: He reconciles us to God if we believe in him. We are saved because the man—Christ, Jesus—took our sin upon himself and was crucified. For Paul, for John Wesley, and for millions of men and women through the ages, this fact has powerfully transformed lives.

In the eighteenth century, as in our own time, many Christians took this saving grace for granted. John Wesley was enraged by the complacency about the cross of Christ within his own Anglican tradition. A prevailing attitude in the 1700's was that all that could be said about the crucifixion of Jesus had been said; it was time to address weightier matters. For John Wesley, there was no weightier matter.

Wesley felt that it was imperative for Christian believers to understand what God did for them through Jesus Christ. He felt that, without this depth of understanding, a person would not likely be truly and deeply changed. Wesley was concerned that so many people called themselves Christian but displayed no outward sign of inward change. Around this concern, Wesley developed his vision of personal (scriptural) holiness.

Personal holiness can be understood as a bridge between the conversion of the individual to the Christian faith and perfection—the understanding that sin has been completely rooted out of the individual by the grace of God. Perfection is understood not as doing nothing wrong but as a gift from God that breaks through the ordinary to encourage and transform the individual. For Wesley, all of life was a moving on toward perfection. Personal holiness is not works righteousness. We do not make ourselves perfect, but we make ourselves ready for the perfection that God will reveal in us.

In his sermon "The Circumcision of the Heart," Wesley describes the basis of personal holiness to be humility, faith, hope, and charity. Combined with the instruction given in "The Means of Grace" and other sermons, Wesley offered a prescription for a life of holiness. Wesley believed that the mission of the church is "to spread scriptural holiness across the land." The church needed men and women who would strive toward perfection—justified, sanctified, and practicing the means of grace in an attitude of personal holiness.

Corporate Holiness and the Kingdom of God

Wesley contended that if individuals would commit to adopting a holy life, the kingdom of God would emerge upon the earth. However, an individual could not live the life of personal holiness without support. Personal holiness had no meaning apart from corporate holiness.

One of the strongest movements of the nineteenth and early twentieth centuries was the personal pietism movement. Pietism, the commitment to prayer and Bible study for growth in faith and devotion, began in Germany in the late 1600's. Two centuries later, its nature had shifted from the corporate sphere to the individual sphere. Although faith had always been a personal matter, through the evolution of the pietism movement, faith became both personal and *private*. Especially in the North American experience, characterized by "rugged individualism," Christianity became less community-based and more personally centered. A survey of hymnody through the period reveals a distinct movement from the corporate ("O God *our* help in ages past...", "Now thank we all *our* God...") to the individual ("Blessed assurance, Jesus is *mine*...", "*I* walk through the garden *alone*..."). The implications of this shift were not readily apparent, and the ultimate breakdown of Christian community and fellowship was not anticipated. It is obvious that Wesley never entertained the notion that the pursuit of personal holiness might ultimately undermine the church.

It was inconceivable to Wesley that there could exist a church where men and women would gather together to worship on a Sunday morning and have no meaningful contact the rest of the week. To worship, people needed to be linked together by spirit and life experience. Christian community was where lives were knit together, where people shared their deepest yearnings and hopes, their greatest desires and dreams. Church was not a place where people came to get something but a place where people came to *be* something. People came to church seeking Jesus, and they most often found him in the kindness and care of the women and men of the congregation. Newcomers were invited to join the journey toward holiness. No one walked that path alone.

The course of privatized religion experienced by most mainline Protestants (most prevalent in white congregations) is disheartening. Very few of Jesus' teachings were directed to individuals. Jesus and Paul both used the plural "you" when offering instruction. Paul spoke to communities. The church for eighteen centuries operated out of a community paradigm. Only now, looking back, can we begin to see what we have lost by individualizing the Christian faith. The church of the future is a church that will reestablish community as its base and that will build connections to enable people to support and encourage one another on the pathway to personal holiness.

A Reflective Moment Along the Way

Reread the last sentence above. If this is true, what will it take for us to make it happen? What concrete steps would have to be put into place for the true congregational transformation of the church from activity center to a community that will build connections among people and between people and God?

List three concrete steps necessary for such a transformation to be realized. Think "outside the box," and keep your focus on growing disciples. Be prepared to tell about your ideas in your Faith-Quest group.

Key Concepts for the Journey
Quality Versus Excellence

C.J.'s barbecue ribs are quality. The meat is perfectly cooked; the sauce is superb; and you never have to worry about getting a bad meal. Consistency is a given. C.J.'s exceeds expectations and delights people every time. But the C.J.'s dining experience is not excellent. C.J.'s is a hole in the wall by the White River. The outside of the building is dirty. The tables wobble, and there is dirt on the floor. The menus are stained with sauce and grease. Food comes on a paper plate, and drinks come from a cooler. C.J. is a large, gruff man who tolerates no chitchat. People who frequent C.J.'s go for the ribs, then they get going. C.J. makes his ribs; if you like them, fine; and if you don't, that's fine, too. No one thinks of C.J.'s as an excellent dining experience. But C.J.'s ribs are quality ribs.

Quality and *excellence* are not the same, even though we often use the words interchangeably. Quality is a subjective standard, existing along a broad spectrum from "superior" to "poor." Excellence is an objective standard. "Poor quality" makes sense, while "poor excellence" does not.

We may provide a service that meets the standard of excellence, but if it doesn't delight the customer, it's not quality. Conversely, something that delights the customer might meet no objective standard of excellence. Excellence is defined by the producers of the goods or services; quality is defined by the customer.

Often in our churches, we strive for excellence and call it quality. We set high standards for worship, music, Sunday school, preaching, and a dozen other church activities; and we pride ourselves on the results. However, this excellence translates to quality only when it meets the needs of the people in the pews and then exceeds their expectations and delights them.

A conversation with young couples in their twenties and thirties at a Nashville, Tennessee, United Methodist church revealed the following information. Of twenty-seven young adults questioned, nine said they were looking for a place to meet other Christians; seven said they wanted to find a small group for study and prayer; six claimed that they wanted to sing but didn't like singing to an organ or listening to a choir; five wanted a chance to talk to the pastors about questions of faith; and five wanted to get involved in service projects. No one mentioned worship or preaching, no one talked about Sunday school or serving on committees. All agreed that the church offered excellent programs, but no one was willing to concede that it was a "high-quality" church. In many cases, we have sacrificed quality for excellence; and we are paying a price.

Few people feel the need to improve upon excellence. Once the highest standard is met, there is no need to go further. However, quality is always open to improvement. No matter how good we are, we can be better. Our cultural obsession with excellence has infiltrated the church. The Christian life becomes destination bound: We want to finish on top, to be the best, to be perfect. Yet the goal of the Christian faith is not a destination but a process of continuous growth.

When John Wesley spoke of going on to perfection, he was speaking in terms of quality, not excellence. Perfection was not a destination. Wesley was promoting a process of spiritual development rather than a standard of attainment. He challenged the idea that Christian perfection was a prize to be won. The Anglican church of Wesley's day had made it just that. If a person prayed daily, attended church weekly, gave to the church and the poor fund, and slipped the priest a little on the side, then that man or woman was indeed considered an excellent Christian. Although he did not use our terminology, Wesley questioned whether being an "excellent" Christian was the same as being a "quality" Christian.

Going on to perfection required personal holiness. Personal holiness was a process that began in the transformed heart, spread throughout the "new-born" human being, and emanated in the thoughts, words, and actions of the individual in Christian love. True Christians could be detected by the different ways they talked and acted. The true Christian was always striving to improve, to learn, to grow. The true Christian had no choice but to serve others. The true Christian witnessed to the power and truth of Jesus Christ without uttering a word. Christians were known by their fruits. Christians defined quality.

The best way to help others move on to perfection is for the church to model that process. Excellence does not always ensure quality. Striving to provide the "best" music, the "best" preaching, the "best" teaching, the "best" anything may keep us from transforming lives. We may well hand out stones and scorpions to those seeking fish and bread. The only people who can define quality for us are the people we serve, so we must learn to listen. Until we hear what people are seeking, how do we really know what to provide?

Empowerment

Empowerment means "to grant authority to change." It is not the responsibility of the church to change lives, but it is the responsibility of those in leadership to give authority and permission to the people to have their lives changed. God in Jesus Christ is the only one who can truly change lives. People do not come to church to be changed; but most deeply desire to change, to be better than they are.

People do not resist change; they resist being changed. One teenager said of his church, "I don't like it because they keep telling me who to be and how to act. They don't know me, they don't seem to want to know me, and they act as if they don't like people like me. I don't want them to try to make me different. I want them to help me know who I really am." Empowerment is the way that we help people find out who they really are, who God made them to be.

Empowerment takes the pressure off us to decide how people must change. No longer do we participate in "cookie-cutter" Christianity, where we strive to make each person like everyone else. We stop setting up false standards, and we stop measuring people to see if they "belong." This allows leaders to lead in a different way. Leadership isn't about dragging people kicking and screaming to where we want them. It is about empowering people to go where God is calling them. Empowerment is a way of bringing everyone together, thus forming true community.

We live in a disempowering world. The world is too big, and the problems are overwhelming. We are pressured to buy things, wear the latest clothes, eat trendy foods, and know all kinds of information. Many people feel helpless. Sensing that they have no control in their lives, people are seeking help. The church can offer help to the people who need it most. The church provides the stability and sanity of God to a chaotic and struggling world.

Questions for Discussion

What are people seeking when they come to your church on Sunday morning? What brings them to church at other times through the week?

In what ways do you confuse excellence and quality? Where in your church are people receiving true quality? How can you improve quality for the people you serve?

How do you empower people to discover who they really are and who God calls them to be? What are you doing in your congregation that may, in fact, be disempowering?

_____

_____

_____

_____

_____

Discovery
Naming Our Current Reality

Many of us live our lives in ways that prevent us from being happy and fulfilled. One of the most common ways is that we attempt to live up to the unrealistic expectations of our society, our neighbors, our families, and even ourselves. We set standards for success, popularity, wealth, and beauty that are beyond our control. Then we direct all our resources toward achieving these ends; and when they remain elusive, we despair.

Determining which things in life are within our control and which are not is essential. As leaders in a congregation, it is important to understand what we can and cannot do.

The following exercise is intended to provide a framework to help clarify what leaders can and cannot do.

Exercise

Figure 16A illustrates three domains in which we live.[36] The large rectangle represents reality. The large oval inside the rectangle is our experience space—that portion of reality that we encounter throughout our lives. This includes all that we learn, everyone we meet, all the information we encounter, the larger society in which we live. The smaller circle within the oval is our control space—the zone where we can make decisions and take actions without help, influence, or restriction from any outside source.

We have no control over the part of reality with which we do not interact. We have limited control

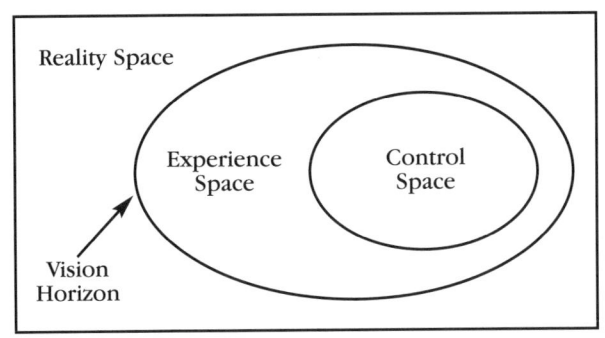

Figure 16A

over our experience space; and it takes a great deal of time, attention, and energy to change things in this sphere. However, we are completely in charge of our control space. This is where we can focus our attention to grow, to improve, to learn, and to adapt. At the very center of our control space is our relationship with God in Jesus Christ. Also within our control space are our skill development, our relationships with others, our attitudes, our self-awareness, and our lifestyle choices.

In our control space, we can focus on our spiritual gifts; the means of grace; the integration of discipleship, stewardship, and fellowship. We can make space for God to work with us to expand the parameters of our control space. The media, science and technology, business, schools, and politics are all working to expand our experience space. As experience space expands, control space shrinks. No one is working to expand our control space for us. On the outer rim of our experience space is our vision horizon. The vision horizon is the personal vision we hold for our lives. It is our greatest hope, our deepest yearning, the way we want to be known in the world. We move closer to that vision as we expand our control space and decrease the gap between control and experience.

By attending to things within our control space, we expand that space. We develop skills or knowledge, and we are better able to cope with life. When we turn attention inward, growing in self-awareness, we turn attention away from our experience space, thus reducing it. If we decide to simplify our lifestyle, then the pressures of culture to buy, buy, buy diminish. If we learn a new skill, then we have one less unknown in our experience space. When we focus on God, we ignore the lesser gods of culture. Control space increases, experience space decreases, and we move closer to our vision for our lives.

Use Figure 16B to identify three specific, measurable things you will do to expand your control space in the weeks and months ahead. The last column suggests we report weekly progress to a prayer partner. Wesley understood this model of

Figure 16B

EXAMPLE	READ MATTHEW EVERY MORNING FOR 15 MINUTES FOR A MONTH	BEGINNING MONDAY, MAY 1	ENDING THURSDAY, JUNE 1	REPORT WEEKLY PROGRESS TO PRAYER PARTNER
1.				
2.				
3.				

accountable discipleship as necessary because we need others to help us wrestle with expanding our control space. This was a common experience within Wesley's Class Meetings. With this in mind, answer the following questions.

How can you help people in your church expand their control space? What do you do in your congregation that expands people's experience space without expanding their control space—thus disempowering them? How can you change those processes?

For Resources, Teaching Aids, and Newest Information

Check out our website at www.faithquest.net.

SESSION 17:
The World Is Our Parish

Key Wesleyan Concepts:
- The scope of our mission
- A vision for fulfilling our mission
- The transformation of the world into the kingdom of God

Key Concepts for the Journey:
- Models of the church
- Synergy
- Strategic planning

Outline:
- Gathering
- A Time of Centering
- Prayer
- Preparation
  Questions and Answers
- Exploration
  Questions and Small-Group Exercises
- Discovery
- Conclusion
- A Celebration of Our FaithQuest Journey
  Closing Worship

Introduction

This session provides a summary and review of much that has gone before. We will revisit topics such as mission and vision, leadership, systems and processes, and continuous improvement. We will celebrate who we are and who God is calling us to be. We will consider that no matter how faithfully we are serving, we can do more to honor and glorify God. Let us rejoice in being the church, the body of Christ. Let us give thanks to God.

Prayer

Gracious Lord, hold us in your loving arms, and lift us in your strength for the work you are calling us to do. We are so grateful for the opportunity to serve you and neighbors. We feel so good about the many ways we faithfully work through your church. We are excited by a vision for the future, for new possibilities and new directions. We are encouraged by a new way of thinking about you, about the church, about the world, and about our communal Christian life. May we do all in our power to grow into the fullness of your vision for us, individually and as your church. We praise you, in our Savior's name. Amen.

Preparation
Daily Reading and Questions for Reflection

Day 1 — excerpt from John Wesley's Journal (June 11, 1739)[37]

Permit me to speak plainly. If by Catholic principles you mean any other than Scriptural, they weigh nothing with me: I allow no other rule, whether of faith or practice, than the Holy Scriptures: But on scriptural principles, I do not think it hard to justify whatever I do. God in Scripture commands me, according to my power, to instruct the ignorant, reform the wicked, confirm the virtuous. Man forbids me to do this in another's parish; that is, in effect, to do it at all; seeing I have now no parish of my own, nor probably ever shall. Whom then shall I hear, God or man? "If it be just to obey man rather than God, judge you. A dispensation of the Gospel is committed to me; and woe is me, if I preach not the Gospel." But where shall I preach it, upon the principles you mention? Why, not in Europe, Asia, Africa, or America; not in any of the Christian parts, at least, of the habitable earth. For all these are, after a sort, divided into parishes. If it be said, "Go back, then, to the Heathens from whence you came:" Nay, but neither could I now (on your principles) preach to them; for all the Heathens in Georgia belong to the parish either of Savannah or Frederica.

Suffer me now to tell you my principles in this matter. I look upon all the world as my parish; thus far I mean, that, in whatever part of it I am, I judge it meet, right, and my bounden duty, to declare unto all that are willing to hear, the glad tidings of salvation. This is the work which I know God has called me to; and sure I am, that his blessing attends it. Great encouragement have I, therefore, to be faithful in fulfilling the work He hath given me to do. His servant I am, and, as such, am employed according to the plain direction of his word, "As I have opportunity, doing good unto all men:" And his providence clearly concurs with his word; which has disengaged me from all things else, that I might singly attend on this very thing, "and go about doing good."

Question: What does it mean for your congregation to view the whole world as its parish? Does your church assist people in accomplishing the work that God calls them to do?

Scripture Reflection: Matthew 25:34-40
How has Jesus "come" to your congregation? In whom? For what? How well do you know the community around your church?

What would need to happen for your congregation to find meaning in using their gifts and graces to help transform people's lives?

_____

_____

_____

_____

Day 2 — excerpt from John Wesley's sermon "The General Spread of the Gospel"[38]

At that time will be accomplished all those glorious promises made to the Christian Church, which will not then be confined to this or that nation, but will include all the inhabitants of the earth. "They shall not hurt nor destroy in all my holy mountain." (Isaiah xi.9.) "Violence shall no more be heard in thy land, wasting nor destruction within thy borders; but thou shalt call thy walls Salvation, and thy gates Praise." Thou shalt be encompassed on every side with salvation, and all that go through thy gates shall praise God. "The sun shall be no more thy light by day; neither for brightness shall the moon give light unto thee: But the Lord shall be unto thee an everlasting light, and thy God thy glory." The light of the sun and the moon shall be swallowed up in the light of His countenance, shining upon thee. "Thy people also shall be all righteous, ... the work of my hands, that I may be glorified." "As the earth bringeth forth her bud, and the garden causeth the things that are sown in it to spring forth; so the Lord God will cause righteousness and praise to spring forth before all the nations." (Isaiah lx.18, &c.; and lxi.11.)

This I apprehend to be the answer, yea, the only full and satisfactory answer that can be given, to the objection against the wisdom and goodness of God, taken from the present state of the world. It will not always be thus: These things are only permitted for a season by the great Governor of the world, that he may draw immense, eternal good out of this temporary evil. This is the very key which the Apostle himself gives us in the words above recited: "God hath concluded them all in unbelief, that he might have mercy upon all." In view of this glorious event, how well may we cry out, "O the depth of the riches both of the wisdom and knowledge of God!" although for a season "his judgments were unsearchable, and his ways past finding out." (Rom xi.32, 33.) It is enough, that we are assured of this one point, that all these transient evils will issue well; will have a happy conclusion; and that "mercy first and last will reign." All unprejudiced persons may see with their eyes, that He is already renewing the face of the earth: And we have strong reason to hope that the work he hath begun, he will carry on unto the day of the Lord Jesus; that he will never intermit this blessed work of his Spirit, until he has fulfilled all his promises, until he hath put a period to sin, and misery, and infirmity, and death, and re-established universal holiness and happiness, and caused all the inhabitants of the earth to sing together, "Hallelujah, the Lord God omnipotent reigneth!" "Blessing, and glory, and wisdom, and honour, and power, and might, be unto our God for ever and ever!" (Rev. vii.12.)

Question: What is Wesley's vision for God's kingdom on earth? How can you participate in the realization of such a vision?

Scripture Reflection: Luke 4:16-21
As Jesus lifts up the text from the Prophet Isaiah, what can you say about Jesus' vision of the kingdom of God? What is the shared vision of your church currently? What might it become?

_____

_____

_____

_____

_____

Day 3 — excerpt from John Wesley's sermon "A Single Intention"[39]

"What reward then will ye give unto the Lord, for all the benefits he hath done unto you?" What? Why, give him your hearts; love him with all your souls; serve him with all your strength. Forget the things that are behind: riches, honour, power—in a word, whatever does not lead to God. Behold, all things about you are become new! Be ye likewise new creatures! From this hour at least let your eye be single: whatever ye speak, or think, or do, let God be your aim, and God only! Let your one end be to please and love God! In all your business, all your refreshments, all your diversions, all your conversations, as well as in all those which are commonly called religious duties, let your eye look straight forward to God. He that hath ears to hear, let him hear! Have one design, one desire, one hope! Even that the God whom we serve may be your God and your all, in time and in eternity! O be not of a double heart! Think of nothing else! Seek nothing else! To love God, and to be beloved by him, is enough. Be your eyes fixed on this one point, and your whole bodies shall be full of light. God shall continually lift up, and that more and more, the light of his countenance upon you. His Holy Spirit shall dwell in you, and shine more and more upon your souls unto the perfect day. He shall purify your hearts by faith from every earthly thought, every unholy affection. He shall establish your souls with so lively a hope as already lays hold on the prize of your high calling. He shall fill you with peace, and joy, and love! Love, the brightness of his glory, the express image of his person! Love which never rests, never faileth, but still spreads its flame, still goeth on conquering and to conquer, till what was but now a weak, foolish, wavering, sinful creature, be filled with all the fullness of God!

Question: In what ways would your life change if you took seriously Wesley's instruction to let your "one end be to please and love God"?

Scripture Reflection: Romans 12:9-18
Could this passage become a model for such a life? Why or why not?

_____

_____

_____

_____

_____

Day 4 — Theological Guidelines: Sources and Criteria[40]

As United Methodists, we have an obligation to bear a faithful Christian witness to Jesus Christ, the living reality at the center of the Church's life and witness. To fulfill this obligation, we reflect

149

FaithQuest: A New Way of Thinking About the Christian Life

critically on our biblical and theological inheritance, striving to express faithfully the witness we make in our own time.

Two considerations are central to this endeavor: the sources from which we derive our theological affirmations and the criteria by which we assess the adequacy of our understanding and witness.

Wesley believed that the living core of the Christian faith was revealed in Scripture, illumined by tradition, vivified in personal experience, and confirmed by reason.

Scripture is primary, revealing the Word of God "so far as it is necessary for our salvation." Therefore, our theological task, in both its critical and constructive aspects, focuses on disciplined study of the Bible.

To aid his study of the Bible and deepen his understanding of faith, Wesley drew on Christian tradition, in particular the Patristic writings, the ecumenical creeds, the teachings of the Reformers, and the literature of contemporary spirituality.

Thus, tradition provides both a source and a measure of authentic Christian witness, though its authority derives from its faithfulness to the biblical message.

The Christian witness, even when grounded in Scripture and mediated by tradition, is ineffectual unless understood and appropriated by the individual. To become our witness, it must make sense in terms of our own reason and experience.

For Wesley, a cogent account of the Christian faith required the use of reason, both to understand Scripture and to relate the biblical message to wider fields of knowledge. He looked for confirmations of the biblical witness in human experience, especially the experiences of regeneration and sanctification, but also in the "common sense" knowledge of everyday experience.

The interaction of these sources and criteria in Wesley's own theology furnishes a guide for our continuing theological task as United Methodists. In that task Scripture, as the constitutive witness to the wellsprings of our faith, occupies a place of primary authority among these theological sources.

In practice, theological reflection may also find its point of departure in tradition, experience, or rational analysis. What matters most is that all four guidelines be brought to bear in faithful, serious, theological consideration. Insights arising from serious study of the Scriptures and tradition enrich contemporary experience. Imaginative and critical thought enables us to understand better the Bible and our common Christian history.

Question: How do Scripture, tradition, experience, and reason provide us with everything necessary to live effective, faithful lives as Christian disciples?

Scripture Reflection:
Search the Book of Psalms to find a psalm that expresses the way you feel as you consider the wonder of God's transforming and creative power and grace.

_____

_____

_____

_____

_____

_____

Day 5 — The Ministry of All Christians[41]

¶126. *The Ministry of the Community*—The church as the community of the new covenant has participated in Christ's ministry of grace across the years and around the world. It stretches out to human needs wherever love and service may convey God's love and ours. The outreach of such ministries knows no limits. Beyond the diverse forms of ministry is this ultimate concern: that all persons will be brought into a saving relationship with God through Jesus Christ and be renewed after the image of their creator (Colossians 3:10). This means that all Christians are called to minister wherever Christ would have them serve and witness in deeds and words that heal and free.

¶127. *Ministry as Gift and Task*—This ministry of all Christians in Christ's name and spirit is both a gift and a task. The gift is God's unmerited grace; the task is unstinting service. Entrance into the church is acknowledged in baptism and may include persons of all ages. In this sacrament the church claims God's promise, the seal of the Spirit (Ephesians 1:13). Baptism is followed by nurture and the consequent awareness by the baptized of the claim to ministry in Christ placed upon their lives by the church. Such a ministry is ratified in confirmation, where the pledges of baptism are accepted and renewed for life and mission. Entrance into and acceptance of ministry begin in a local church, but the impulse to minister always moves one beyond the congregation toward the whole human community. God's gifts are richly diverse for a variety of services; yet all have dignity and worth.

¶128. *Faithful Ministry*—The people of God, who are the church made visible in the world, must convince the world of the reality of the gospel or leave it unconvinced. There can be no evasion or delegation of this responsibility; the church is either faithful as a witnessing and serving community, or it loses its vitality and its impact on an unbelieving world.

Question: How do these paragraphs from the *Book of Discipline* illuminate, clarify, and expand your understanding of the mission "to make disciples of Jesus Christ"?

_____
_____
_____
_____
_____
_____

Day 6 — Our Social Creed[42]

We believe in God, Creator of the world; and in Jesus Christ, the Redeemer of creation. We believe in the Holy Spirit, through whom we acknowledge God's gifts, and we repent of our sin in misusing these gifts to idolatrous ends.

We affirm the natural world as God's handiwork and dedicate ourselves to its preservation, enhancement, and faithful use by humankind.

We joyfully receive for ourselves and others the blessings of community, sexuality, marriage, and the family.

We commit ourselves to the rights of men, women, children, youth, young adults, the aging, and people with disabilities; to improvement of the quality of life; and to the rights and dignity of racial, ethnic, and religious minorities.

We believe in the right and duty of persons to work for the glory of God and the good of themselves and others and in the protection of their welfare in so doing; in the rights to property as a trust from God, collective bargaining, and responsible consumption; and in the elimination of economic and social distress.

We dedicate ourselves to peace throughout the world, to the rule of justice and law among nations, and to individual freedom for all people of the world.

We believe in the present and final triumph of God's Word in human affairs and gladly accept our commission to manifest the life of the gospel in the world. Amen.

Question: Reflect on the above affirmations from "Our Social Creed." How do you as an individual practice these beliefs and commitments? How does your congregation practice these beliefs and commitments? Are there any aspects of "Our Social Creed" that we ignore or deny?

Read the session material and make notes in the margin.

_____
_____
_____
_____
_____
_____

Exploration
Background Information: The Scope of Our Mission

The mission of The United Methodist Church has been defined as "making disciples of Jesus Christ."

It is important to remember that the passage from Matthew from which this instruction is taken actually reads, "Go therefore and make disciples of all nations, baptizing them in the name of the Father and of the Son and of the Holy Spirit, and teaching them to obey everything that I have commanded you" (Matthew 28:19-20). We need to be careful not to narrow the scope of our mission as we are now entering a truly global millennium. Our mission is not to make disciples of just those who enter our doors. It is, first, to "go." Then it is to extend that mission to "all nations." John Wesley would call us to broaden our mission and to remember that we are serving a larger cause than disciple-making.

John Wesley responded to criticism of his ministry in the open air by announcing "the world is my parish." For Wesley, the church extended into the world in the person of every man, woman, and child who held Christ in his or her heart. The work of the church was not a Sunday event but a lifestyle. Disciple-making was not a function of the institution but a by-product of faithful Christians living fully in the world. One could not help being touched by the power-filled lives of Christian men and women.

We want to be careful not to confuse the institutional mission of disciple-making with the larger, ongoing mission of transforming the world into the kingdom of God. God is performing this miracle through all God's people all the time. For The United Methodist Church, we have determined that the best way our denomination can participate in the Kingdom-building vision is to dedicate ourselves to making disciples. Once more, it is a good idea to reflect on the instruction "go" and the inclusive scope of "all nations."

A Vision for Fulfilling Our Mission

The faith-forming communities of the twenty-first century will be dynamic, active bodies that are not tied to place or physical structures. Reclaiming the early missionary sense of Jesus and Paul, the church must have a vital presence in the world. As one young man reflected, "The church can't act like a Venus's flytrap, waiting for fresh meat to happen by. If it does, it's going to die." Passivity is a mark of the past. The church of the future will go where it is needed.

We need to recognize that the identity of the church has already shifted. We are a global church. The influx of Hispanic, Korean, African, Pacific Islander, and Caribbean Islander Christians (just to name a few) is on the rise. Methodism in Africa, South and Central America, Korea, the former Eastern Bloc states, and Cambodia is booming. Developing nations are on fire with the power and presence of God's Holy Spirit. All around the world, there are pockets of the kind of evangelical fire that sparked the birth of Methodism. In the United States, we have much to learn about being the church from these younger brother and sister congregations. However, we cannot learn from them if they remain outside our experience. We must learn an entirely new language of connectionalism to be relevant in the new century.

The Transformation of the World

If we are to be relevant in the new century, we need a new understanding of missions. Mission is no longer what we engage in "over there, for those people." We are one *United* Methodist Church, united Christians participating in the unfolding of God's eternal kingdom. We are disciples and stewards together in one world fellowship. The vision that John Wesley only hinted at more than two hundred years ago is the reality today. Our mission is for the entire world, not just for our local congregation in our small corner of the planet.

We have become so institutionally minded in the activity-center paradigm that we focus more on self-preservation than on growth and transformation. Because many United Methodist churches are in a survival mode, we are oblivious to the incredible explosion of spirit and new life; and we are ill-prepared to enter the faith-forming-community paradigm. We need to seek God's guidance and ask God to help us find our place in this modern-day miracle. There is more than enough to do. As we tap into the flow of energy and life cascading through our church, we will find renewal at home. People are looking for the kingdom of God. We have a beautiful opportunity to present it to them, if only we will acknowledge the changing world and be flexible.

JESUS MODEL OF THE CHURCH	PAULINE MODEL OF THE CHURCH
Mobile	Stationary
Small cell groups	Congregational
Organic	Mechanistic
Spirit-led	Gifts-based
Apostolic	Ecclesial
Teacher—Disciple	Shepherd—Flock
"Just in Time"	Fixed days and times

Figure 17A

Key Concepts for the Journey
Models of the Church

To find an appropriate model for the church of the twenty-first century, we need look no further than the New Testament. The gospels and the letters of Paul present two powerful, missionary models of the church: the Jesus model and the Pauline model.

The church model of Jesus Christ was mobile, not tied to any one location. The church went where the people were. It consisted of a leader surrounded by a small group of followers. It was organic, changing from time to time, following a loose structure. Teaching, healing, and preaching occurred as needs arose. Prayer was central to the life of the church; and as the Spirit led, the church was moved to follow. It was always moving into a new situation, into a new setting, seeking a new audience. The model was based upon a teacher-disciple relationship.

The Pauline model differed in a number of respects. Paul planted churches wherever he went. He tied congregations to locations. There were specific gathering points, and there were rituals and structures immediately set into place. The preaching, the teaching, the healing became part of the community life. The church found identity and definition around worship and ritual practice. The design of the church structure was gifts-based, and it followed a shepherd-flock model, where one or a few led the entire congregation. It was a more hierarchical structure. These two church models are illustrated in Figure 17A.

Churches today resemble the Pauline model much more closely than the Jesus model. It would be presumptuous to assume that we need to return to the Jesus model. When Paul modified the image of the church, he did so with integrity. Paul did not think he was replacing the Jesus model but thought he was improving or completing it. What is needed for the twenty-first century is not one or the other but a synthesis of the two.

The congregation that can be most relevant for our day is one that both is mobile and offers a gathering point. Its ministries are housed within the church and are present outside the church. While we are inviting people in, we are also sending people out to share the good news. We work all aspects of the primary task concurrently. We renew our commitment to a gifts-based ministry, and we center the work that we do in prayer and in the practice of the other means of grace. We structure to support the people. We see our mission out in the world; we gather in communion to build a true fellowship that empowers our outreach.

The models of the church that have come to us through the ages are still pertinent. They challenge what we have become and encourage us to become something more. Rather than reducing our vision to encompass the Jesus model or the Pauline model, we explore the implications and possibilities afforded by symbiosis.

Synergy

Synergy occurs when the outcome is greater than the sum of the parts. Synergy takes place in the church when we start living together toward the vision that God reveals to us. It occurs when gifted people combine their energy and talent to make something wonderful happen. Synergy happens whenever two or three gather in the presence of God. It is the transcendent reality of God's Holy Spirit at work in our lives. Synergy is the very nature of the church. The fact that synergy occurs so infrequently is a clear sign that something is wrong—that the system is designed for the results it is getting, not the results God intends.

Leaders of local congregations need to decide to synergize and to begin dreaming the faith dreams of God's people. Synergy occurs in learning organizations. It emerges through processes of continuous improvement. Synergy results in spiral flow, which moves upward toward greater quality. Synergy is the product of appropriate systems, where all processes are aligned toward the desired outcome. Synergy tells us that we are on the right track. Synergy is possible for churches that embrace the full potential of the faith-forming-community paradigm.

Strategic Planning

Strategic planning allows leaders to determine the desired outcome and then work backward to determine how to accomplish the outcome. What it costs, how much time it will take, how many people it requires, how much energy it takes, where it ought to happen—all are based on the desired outcome. When we begin to design our systems for ministry, let's use strategic planning and begin with the end in mind. The whole process looks something like Figure 17B.

Too often, we design our systems before we know who and what we have to work with, what we want to accomplish, and what our purpose really is. Unless we put first things first, we will never be effective at designing the systems for ministry that will allow us to lead in the twenty-first century.

Questions for Discussion

What are the implications of a "world parish" for your congregation? How will people in your church respond to such a concept? How can you communicate the emerging paradigms for your church in an affirming, nonthreatening way? What will happen if we fail?

How can you enable members and friends of your congregation to find a place in the ministry of your church?

How can you extend the influence of your congregation into your community? Into the nation? Around the world?

_____

_____

_____

_____

_____

Discovery
Naming Our Current Reality

A young boy stood on the beach in North Carolina, watching the waves of the Atlantic Ocean pound along the shore. He looked as far as he could see in both directions. Shaking his head, he turned and began walking away. A man asked him what was wrong. The boy replied, "I can't tell where you're supposed to get in."

Figure 17B

DISCOVER	CLARIFY	DETERMINE	DESIGN
the gifts and passions of the people	the mission and vision of the church	the desired objectives and goals for ministry	appropriate systems for ministry

When faced with so many new ideas, so many changing realities, so many shifting paradigms, we can be overwhelmed and confused about where to "get in." Just like the ocean, there is no right or wrong place. If you choose to swim, you just jump in.

Jumping in is the only way we can take new ideas that expand our experience space, make them our own, and transform our control space. The right starting spot for one leadership team will be wrong for another. Congregational transformation is an ongoing process. It happens in different places at different times in different ways.

Some congregations will begin by focusing on the means of grace; others will study learning organizations; others will learn about systems and processes. Some might reflect on quality, while others take time to discover their spiritual gifts. All are fruitful pursuits.

Some responses will be counterproductive. Doing nothing is counterproductive. To do nothing is to do something deadly. *Doing nothing* will destroy our church.

However, doing too much is also counterproductive. Trying to learn everything too quickly defeats the process of continuous improvement and undermines the integrity of the learning organization. Doing a little of everything perpetuates mediocrity. It is better to focus energy and attention on just one or two fronts.

Another inappropriate response would be to begin the process of redesign too early. We need to learn, to listen, to think, to discuss, and to understand. We need to give ourselves permission to sit in silence, to stop planning, to declare a moratorium on meetings for six months or a year, and to open ourselves to one another and to God. We need to pray together, to read together, to think out loud, and—most of all—to share our dreams.

A Celebration of Our FaithQuest Journey

Light a candle and place it in the center of the group. Let the candle's light represent the presence of God in the midst of your group.

Everyone should remain silent for fifteen minutes to leaf through this Bible study and quietly reflect on this experience. What topics, ideas, and exercises excited or inspired you? What readings from Scripture or from Wesley touched a nerve? Where did you feel energized, enlightened, or challenged? What are you thankful for? What do you hope to see as the next step toward transformation?

Take some brief notes on Figure 17C to help you remember.

After fifteen minutes, invite everyone to join in the prayer that follows.

Figure 17C

CONCEPTS/IDEAS	EXERCISES	SCRIPTURES/READINGS
1.	1.	1.
2.	2.	2.
3.	3.	3.
4.	4.	4.
5.	5.	5.

Closing Worship
Unison Prayer:

Living God of creation, your way is to make all things new. You began by creating the world and saw that it was good. When your children rebelled you never gave up. You never stopped loving them. Indeed, you created a plan to redeem all your children into a new and eternal relationship with you, in and through Jesus Christ. You called each one of us into discipleship, birthing within us various gifts and abilities, each useful for service in your Kingdom.

Thank you, loving God, for bringing us together over these weeks. We have grown closer to one another and closer to you. We have experienced both moments of disorientation and moments when you opened our eyes to discover new and creative ideas to help our church be your church in a world of dire need.

Keep the excitement of our learning alive in whatever ways you would have us live out our discoveries, for the sake of Jesus Christ, who showed us by example how to love the world into new life. Amen.

Scripture Reading and Response:

Luke 5:1-11

The disciples left their nets, boats, and experiences as fishermen behind to follow Jesus. He was to teach them a new way of fishing, this time for people. Allow each participant to offer his or her own response to the questions.

- What do you hear Jesus calling us to leave behind that we might learn a new way of being God's church?
- Name one significant learning that really moved you.
- What was the most surprising or eye-opening thing for you?
- What are you afraid of as we complete this Bible study?

Sing a Hymn

"Lord, You Have Come to the Lakeshore," # 344 in *The United Methodist Hymnal.*

Closing Prayer:

Lord, this portion of our journey has come to an end. Another journey will begin tomorrow, and another one after that. We thank you for such journeys. We thank you for patience and strength in times when we may fear change or feel challenged. We thank you for the opportunity to develop new relationships and new insights. As we move on to the next step of transformation, help us to never stop asking questions or trying to learn more. Keep our eyes open so that we can be change ready and discover new and creative ways to meet the needs of those you have called us to serve in your name. By your grace, make us a people of endless possibility. We pray in Jesus' holy name. Amen.

Extinguish the candle as the closing act of the study, but the beginning of our journey onward. (Some groups may want to celebrate the Lord's Supper or a Love Feast before concluding.)

For Resources, Teaching Aids, and Newest Information

Check out our website at www.faithquest.net.

Endnotes

1. See *The Once and Future Church*, by Loren B. Mead (Alban Institute, 1991), pages 8-29.

2. Refer to *Personal Excellence*, by Ken Blanchard, audiocassette (Simon and Schuster, 1993).

3. From *The Book of Discipline of The United Methodist Church—2000*. Copyright © 2000 by The United Methodist Publishing House; ¶122, page 88. Used by permission.

4. Information on these levels comes from Paul Batalden and the Quality Resource Group of HCA, Nashville, Tennessee.

5. See *Congregational Megatrends*, by C. Jeff Woods (Alban Institute, 1996).

6. These four styles are loosely based on the four personal styles developed by David W. Merrill and Roger Reig in *Personal Styles and Effective Performance* (Chilton Book Company, 1981).

7. From *The Wisdom of Teams*, by Jon R. Katzenbach and Douglas K. Smith (Harvard Business School Press, 1993), page 45.

8. One of the best sources for information on chaos theory is *At Home in the Universe*, by Stuart Kaufmann (Oxford University Press, 1995), pages 3-30.

9. See *Lessons From the Art of Juggling*, by Michael J. Gelb and Tony Buzan (Harmony Books, 1994).

10. Ballroom dancing is to Australia what figure skating is to America. *Strictly Ballroom* (1992) is a powerful parable of paradigm shifts, mission, vision, continuous improvement, and systems and processes.

11. From *A Simpler Way*, by Margaret Wheatley and Myron Kellner-Rogers (Berrett-Koehler Publishers, 1996), page 80.

12. See *Lessons From the New Workplace*, by Margaret Wheatley (CRM Films, 1996).

13. These definitions are excerpted from *Revolutionizing Christian Stewardship for the 21st Century: Lessons From Copernicus*, by Dan R. Dick (Discipleship Resources, 1997), pages 97-101. Used by permission.

14. This exercise does not replace a spiritual-gifts discovery process. Using a gifts discovery inventory is valuable for understanding the gifts and ways to use and develop the gifts. See, for example, *Equipped for Every Good Work: Building a Gifts-Based Church*, by Dan R. Dick and Barbara Miller (Discipleship Resources, 2001).

15. From Sermon 89, "The More Excellent Way," in *The Works of John Wesley*, edited by Thomas Jackson, Volume 7, pages 26-27.

16. From Sermon 89, "The More Excellent Way," in *The Works of John Wesley*, edited by Thomas Jackson, Volume 7, pages 27-28.

17. From Sermon 89, "The More Excellent Way," in *The Works of John Wesley*, edited by Thomas Jackson, Volume 7, pages 29-30.

18. From Sermon 89, "The More Excellent Way," in *The Works of John Wesley*, edited by Thomas Jackson, Volume 7, pages 30-31.

19. From Sermon 89, "The More Excellent Way," in *The Works of John Wesley*, edited by Thomas Jackson, Volume 7, page 33.

20. From Sermon 89, "The More Excellent Way," in *The Works of John Wesley*, edited by Thomas Jackson, Volume 7, pages 35-37.

21. From Merriam Webster's Collegiate Dictionary, 10th edition (Merriam-Webster, Inc., 1993).

22. *Fellowship* has been challenged as a "sexist" term. Etymologically, the term comes from an Old Norse word meaning "to lay together, partnership." It has nothing to do with gender.

23. From Sermon 16, "The Means of Grace," in *The Works of John Wesley*, edited by Thomas Jackson, Volume 5, pages 185-188.

24. From Sermon 16, "The Means of Grace," in *The Works of John Wesley*, edited by Thomas Jackson, Volume 5, pages 188-189.

25. From Sermon 16, "The Means of Grace," in *The Works of John Wesley*, edited by Thomas Jackson, Volume 5, pages 190-191.

26. From Sermon 16, "The Means of Grace," in *The Works of John Wesley*, edited by Thomas Jackson, Volume 5, pages 192-193.

27. From Sermon 16, "The Means of Grace," in *The Works of John Wesley*, edited by Thomas Jackson, Volume 5, pages 194-195.

28 From Sermon 16, "The Means of Grace," in *The Works of John Wesley*, edited by Thomas Jackson, Volume 5, pages 198, 200-201.

29 See *The Presence of God in the Christian Life: John Wesley and the Means of Grace*, by Henry H. Knight III (Scarecrow Press, 1992).

30 From Sermon 17, "The Circumcision of the Heart," in *The Works of John Wesley*, edited by Thomas Jackson, Volume 5, pages 202-203.

31 From Sermon 17, "The Circumcision of the Heart," in *The Works of John Wesley*, edited by Thomas Jackson, Volume 5, pages 203-204.

32 From Sermon 17, "The Circumcision of the Heart," in *The Works of John Wesley*, edited by Thomas Jackson, Volume 5, pages 204-205.

33 From Sermon 17, "The Circumcision of the Heart," in *The Works of John Wesley*, edited by Thomas Jackson, Volume 5, pages 205-206.

34 From Sermon 17, "The Circumcision of the Heart," in *The Works of John Wesley*, edited by Thomas Jackson, Volume 5, pages 207-208.

35 From Sermon 17, "The Circumcision of the Heart," in *The Works of John Wesley*, edited by Thomas Jackson, Volume 5, pages 211-212.

36 These concepts are based in part on the work of Edward de Bono in *The Happiness Purpose* (Penguin Books, 1977).

37 From *The Journal of John Wesley*, in *The Works of John Wesley*, edited by Thomas Jackson, Volume 1, pages 201-202.

38 From Sermon 63, "The General Spread of the Gospel," in *The Works of John Wesley*, edited by Thomas Jackson, Volume 6, pages 287-288.

39 From Sermon 148, "A Single Intention," in *The Works of John Wesley*, Volume 4, Sermons IV: 115–151, edited by Albert C. Outler (Abingdon Press, 1987), pages 376-377.

40 From "Our Theological Task," in *The Book of Discipline of The United Methodist Church*—2000. Copyright © 2000 by The United Methodist Publishing House; ¶104, pages 76-77. Used by permission.

41 From "The Mission and Ministry of the Church," Section II, "The Ministry of All Christians," in *The Book of Discipline of The United Methodist Church*—2000. Copyright © 2000 by The United Methodist Publishing House; ¶¶126-128, pages 89-90. Used by permission.

42 From "Social Principles," VII, "Our Social Creed," in *The Book of Discipline of The United Methodist Church*—2000. Copyright © 2000 by The United Methodist Publishing House; ¶166, page 122. Used by permission.